KOREANS IN IRAN

KOREANS IN IRAN

MISSILES, MARKETS AND MYTHS

SHIRZAD AZAD

Algora Publishing
New York

Library of Congress Cataloging-in-Publication Data —

Names: Azad, Shirzad, author.
Title: Koreans in Iran : missiles, markets, and myths / Shirzad Azad.
Description: New York : Algora Publishing, [2018] | Includes bibliographical
    references and index.
Identifiers: LCCN 2018014299 (print) | LCCN 2018018770 (ebook) | ISBN
    9781628943351 (pdf) | ISBN 9781628943337 (soft cover : alk. paper) | ISBN
    9781628943344 (hard cover : alk. paper)
Subjects: LCSH: Iran—Foreign relations—Korea (South) | Korea
    (South)—Foreign relations—Iran. | Iran—Foreign relations—Korea (North)
    | Korea (North)—Foreign relations—Iran.
Classification: LCC DS274.2.K6 (ebook) | LCC DS274.2.K6 A93 2018 (print) |
    DDC 303.48/2550519—dc23
LC record available at https://lccn.loc.gov/2018014299

Printed in the United States

Table of Contents

PREFACE

This study takes on the surprising riddle of Korea–Iran relations in contemporary history. It starts by examining the many ways that Koreans are active in Iran, despite the nations' seeming dissimilarities, and asks how and why this situation came about.

Koreans have managed to continuously expand their political, economic, and cultural presence in Iran under changing circumstances hovering over the Persian Gulf country. The credit for this significant achievement is not really all due to the Koreans alone, because other influential stakeholders certainly had a role to play as well.

Iranians and Koreans have grudgingly, and often awkwardly, found themselves teamed up in certain international categories, regardless of the prospects of such a linkage under the evolving international circumstances both in the Korean Peninsula and Iran. Despite an abundance of topical questions and pressing issues, the multifaceted Korean–Iranian connection has received very little, if any, attention, scholarly or otherwise. The present research humbly aims to partially fill that critical gap.

In conducting this study, the emphasis is largely placed on an interpretation of reverberations and end results rather than on narratives of events and players. The research also strives to substantiate claims and assertions of all sorts by consulting existing literature in English as well as accessible resources in the Persian and Korean languages. Finally, no one but the author alone bears responsibility for any omission, error, or shortcoming in this work.

— Shirzad Azad

INTRODUCTION

While most Westerners haven't noticed it, Korea is linked with Iran in many different ways, and this has become a major characteristic of Iran's international relations. Koreans themselves find this perplexing. They are flummoxed to see that their nation is, time and again, closely linked to the Iranians one way or another. However, the Iran–Korea affiliation may have even more far-reaching implications for Iranian citizens, both at home and abroad, though most of them have not bothered to ask themselves about it.

The Iranian–Korean association has its own peculiar attributes which differ from the patterns of attachment and alignment seen between Iran and most of its foreign partners. One difference is that ties with Korea seem to pop up in Iran in almost every imaginable aspect, from sensitive political and military areas to delicate economic and cultural spheres. People sometimes ponder why Iranians and Koreans have to team up with each other in so many ways. For instance, in the spheres of economics and technology, the majority of Iranian citizens have recently seen their public and even private lives being increasingly hemmed in by Korean brands and products of every sort, as if their country has been turned into a giant K-Plaza, possibly to the detriment of some interests vital to the normal function of a typical state and conventional society.

A second important feature of the Korea–Iran connection is that Koreans from both sides of the 38ᵗʰ parallel succeed to engage their Iranian counterparts (though the level of engagement with Iran is not equal between North and South Korea). North Koreans associate with Iranians more in the polit-

ical and military sectors, while their controversial and often stigmatic connections to Iran appear to be somewhat haphazard and fraught with twists
and turns.

Quite contrary to the hard politics played by Pyongyang, South Koreans have gained a better reputation for their soft approach toward Iranians
through economic channels and cultural means. Political ideology, even when
it sometimes stems from a third party, plays a pivotal role in the Pyongyang–
Tehran affiliation, but such a key factor is usually absent in Seoul–Tehran
interactions. Of course, South Korea's relationship with Iran has its own peculiar politics, but this factor is normally played down by every stakeholder
in favor of other less contentious areas in economics, finance, technology,
and culture.

Another major component is that Korea's affiliation with modern Iran
has been quite persistent and incremental since the 1950s, both during the
final decades of the Pahlavi dynasty and in the follow-up establishment of
the Islamic Republic.

The stakes were rather high in both periods. Under the Pahlavi monarchy, the Iranian government was once contemplating direct military engagement in a major international conflict over the Korean cause (the Korean
War), while under the Islamic Republic the ostensibly close Iran–North
Korea partnership was never without cost, in one way or another. And there
has been, logically and justifiably, a flurry of social and economic grievances
among Iranians in recent years with regard to South Korea's encroachment
upon their markets and national products. Seoul's pattern of trade balance
and the presence of its indentured construction workers in Tehran during
the final years of Pahlavi monarchy were not really that satisfactory in the
view of Iran, either.

The fourth characteristics of the Korea–Iran affiliation is that Koreans
did not always have to be physically present in Iran to benefit from this dicey
association; certain circumstances unfavorable to Iran sometimes turned out
to be beneficial for Koreans. Examples abound, but here, just two interesting
cases are briefly introduced. Once the Pahlavi monarchy was toppled from
power, a great many of the American weapons for which Iran had paid in full,
in advance, were given to South Korea. This enabled the Korean government
to resell some of them to Tehran on the black market during the early years

of the Iran–Iraq War and charge the Iranians rather handsomely, though the responsibility, or precisely irresponsibility, of the American government is already stark in clarity. In the same way, the quota that had long been allocated to Iranian students at American universities was offered to South Korean students from the early 1980s onward, while other groups of people from the two countries applying for a temporary visa experienced similar contrasting situation.

A last, but not final, element in the Korean–Iranian tango is that these countries have surprisingly little, if anything, in common. Of course, both the Iranian Plateau and the Korean Peninsula are inescapably located in the greater Asian continent, but short of that there is hardly much commonality between the two parties to account for their apparently close relations.

In fact, the riddle of the Korea–Iran affiliation in contemporary history becomes more compelling when one realizes that they have bumped into each other so frequently and so significantly despite their not sharing much politically, economically, and culturally. Koreans, from both sides of the demilitarized zone (DMZ), have built their own socio-political systems as well as techno-economic structures which significantly differ from those found in Iran. Such differences and disparities, however, have not prevented the two sides from engaging in high level interactions. Nor have those obvious dissimilarities really dissuaded some other stakeholders from putting Iranians and Koreans in certain categories and giving them identical labels.

What, then, are the primary political, economic, and cultural connections of Koreans to Iran, and why did these ties come into being? How did Koreans manage to continuously expand their presence in Iran under the changing circumstances hovering over Iran? What forced Iranians and Koreans to grudgingly, and often awkwardly, team up in certain international categories? Do Koreans really deserve to be given all the credit for their significant achievements in Iran? What was the role of other important stakeholders? What will be the prospects of the Iran–Korea affiliation under the current developments unfolding both in the Korean Peninsula and Iran? Despite such questions, why has the multifaceted Korean–Iranian association not received corresponding scholarly attention in policy and particularly academic circles around the world?

The Literature And Its Limitations

By and large, the Korean–Iranian relationship is yet to attract the discussion and scrutiny it deserves among scholars and policymakers. What little research has been done on the topic has, for the most part, been sparse and scattered, but a still bigger problem is that the available literature often suffers from myopic views and partisan perspectives.

While North Korea's interaction with Iran has long inspired pundits and politicians to write passionately about the likely (and even unlikely) implications of Pyongyang–Tehran connections, South Korea's more diverse and sometimes knotty relationship with Iran has not aroused the same attention. Moreover, the scope and net value of North Korean–Iranian relations in both the political and military areas have generally been so highlighted and accentuated, not to say exaggerated, that the economic, and even cultural, exchanges between South Korea and Iran, much larger scope and value, ironically look insignificant. Of course, some of those studies have indubitably been influenced by political or economic agendas, a lack of truly interested experts in the field, cultural differences, language barriers, bureaucratic hurdles, data unavailability, and other problems.

Excepting North Korea, the works produced in South Korea and Iran usually have their own shortcomings as well. When South Koreans write, and even when they talk, about Pyongyang–Tehran connections, the outcome is usually burdened with one or more of the problems adumbrated earlier. The North Korean political system is considered very evil and its relationship with Iran in any area whatsoever is viewed as unlikely to serve the interests of ordinary people in North Korea, let alone the elites of South Korea.

With regard to South Korean–Iranian interactions, the literature penned by writers in the Republic of Korea (ROK) often sounds like some marketing reports produced to serve various vested interests of the Korean conglomerates (chaebol) in Iran, and in fact a great percentage of such works are indeed customized and financed by one or another Korean company. On top of that, in South Korea, the fields of Iranian Studies in particular and Middle East Studies in general still have a long way to go in order to secure their rightful place in top institutions of higher education, and the situation of Korean Studies in Iran is not any better at all. If anything, it is much worse indeed.

In spite of Iran's expanding relations with China, Japan, and the Korean Peninsula over the past decades, academic studies on East Asian countries are yet to produce groundbreaking works commensurate with the Persian Gulf country's overall attention to and vested interest in East Asia. Political science and international relations departments as well as economic and history disciplines have failed to catch up with Iran's significant engagement in East Asia, in part due to a lack of interested and capable specialists.

Although centers for Japanese and Chinese Studies were belatedly established in the humanities or language departments at a number of Iranian national universities, it seems that there is still resistance to commencing a Korean Studies program at a reputable university. In part this problem can also be attributed to an absence of qualified experts in major policymaking bodies and bureaucratic institutions, the Iranian Ministry of Foreign Affairs in particular.

Since the 1950s, almost all political envoys and economic representatives dispatched from Iran to East Asian countries knew very little, if anything at all, about the language and culture of their host society. This of course prevented them from seriously to both engage in and grasp the nuts and bolts of that designated Asian country.

Because of this crucial weakness, some of them could eventually end up serving their host society better rather than their own country which had sent them there on an important diplomatic mission in the first place. And if the foreign ministry failed to receive very timely and accurate reports and assessments about an East Asian country from the diplomats and consuls it dispatched to the region, naturally the relevant committees and departments in the national parliament or other policymaking institutions would not be in a position carve out appropriate plans and policies. This chronic flaw could simply trickle down to many other middle and lower ranking institutions and agencies that had anything to do with that East Asian state. And ordinary Iranian citizens were certainly to be affected as well; an issue which will be further discussed in other chapters.

Plan Of The Book

For better or worse, the Republic of Korea has managed to maintain fairly friendly political ties with Iran uninterruptedly since 1962 despite being a close ally of the United States. In fact, Seoul's political connections to Tehran have never been severed, even when South Korea was astonishingly accused of close collaboration with Washington over the famous Hostage Crisis (November 1979–January 1981) and the botched Operation Eagle Claw (April 1980), the failed attempt to rescue the captured Americans.

In comparison to South Korea, North Korea's political as well as military and security relationship with Iran is no doubt more salient. It started in the 1970s, found its momentous upswing during the Iran–Iraq War (1980–1988), and eventually drew the notorious "Axis of Evil" cliché from President George W. Bush (apparently coined by his speechwriter David Frum) in January 2002. Nowadays hardly a single day elapses without someone harping on the "unsavory" North Korean–Iranian political partnership in the mainstream international media and press, powerful policy circles, or influential academic gatherings.

Economically, the success of South Koreans in Iran is for obvious reasons more dazzling than that of their North Korean brethren. The value of two-way commercial interactions between the ROK and Iran has been ratcheted up remarkably from less than $80 million in 1974 to more than $8 billion this year. Today, South Korea is Iran's third largest imports partner after China and the United Arab Emirates, respectively. But the tiny Arab entrepôt does not produce anything beyond oil, and a great deal of what Seoul ships to Dubai ends up in Iranian markets through official and unofficial channels, making the East Asian country practically the second source of imported goods to Iran.

This fact is encapsulated particularly by the omnipresence of Korean electronic and automobile brands throughout Iranian society. Surveys indicate that some 40 percent of the entire furniture market in Iran is captured by the Korean LG and Samsung companies, while the South Korean chaebol of Kia Motors, Hyundai, and Ssangyang are monopolizing around 60 percent of the whole market of trucks and cars imported into the Persian Gulf country. The market penetration for TV sets and mobile phone devices has been equally phenomenal, turning Iran virtually into a giant K-Plaza.

Culturally, the South Korean movie-making industry has made inroads into Iran during the past decade far beyond the expectations of the Koreans themselves. Iran has become one of the few foreign territories where a number of "Hallyu" products have attracted significant exposure and substantial public attention throughout the country. This achievement is epitomized by the fact that one Korea drama captured higher ratings in Iran than it had already won in its source country, the ROK.

The swift success of Hallyu dramas and serials surprised many cultural connoisseurs inside and outside Iran. In spite of the geographical distance and patent cultural differences between the two countries, this unpredictable outcome was undoubtedly greatly assisted by a whole host of political and economic parameters involving multiple stakeholders. This Hallyu triumph had a knock-on effect, boosting the popularity of Korean brands among Iranian consumers. Additionally, the ROK's cultural publicity in Iran easily outclassed what the Democratic People's Republic of Korea (DPRK) had gained in the Iranian society. After all, the imagined shared "political culture" between the communist state of North Korea and the Islamic Republic has ultimately had little chance to stay on par with the popularity of Hallyu products among their Iranian fans.

The present study is, therefore, organized into three main chapters. The first chapter concentrates on the political, and to some extent military, aspects of the Korean–Iranian connections. After a brief sketch of the intermittent interactions that seem to have taken place between the two parties in ancient times, the chapter then swiftly moves to the late 1950s and early 1960s when Koreans made an attempt to lay the groundwork for the commencement of official long-term relations with Iran in modern history. The chapter later focuses on the post-Pahlavi era when a pivotal and surprising shift in the political and ideological orientation under the newly established regime of the Islamic Republic provided an opportunity for closer ties between Pyongyang and Tehran, while the whole episode forced Seoul to forgo any conspicuous political connection to Iran for a couple of decades. One other important topic in this chapter will be miscellaneous discussions about the dubious role of other stakeholders, the international system in particular, with regard to various crucial twists and turns in the political component of the Korean–Iranian relationship over a period of some seven decades.

The second chapter outlines various areas of Koreans' economic and financial achievements in Iran as well as the prospects of their future presence in the Iranian markets in the aftermath of the nuclear deal signed between Tehran and the 5+1 party (United States, Britain, France, Russia, China, and Germany) in July 2015. Although this chapter does not ignore Pyongyang's rather meager economic exchanges with Tehran, it mainly evaluates the economic presence of South Korea in Iran since the 1960s. Moreover, the chapter takes into account certain domestic developments and important political circumstances in Iran, all of which have crucially influenced the scope and scale of South Korea's economic and financial gains in Iran, particularly over the past decade. For obvious reasons, an integral part of various discussions in this chapter will be frequent references to the external factor (i.e., the international system) and the way it timely and greatly assisted South Koreans in truly making milestones in Iran.

Finally, the third chapter appraises the Korean cultural inroads into the Iranian society. Starting with a brief discussion about the relationship between culture and modern economy, the chapter first looks at the introduction of foreign cultures, including those from the East Asian countries, into contemporary Iran. The chapter then examines the exposure of Iranian society to the Korean wave (Hallyu) by providing detailed explanations of major factors which helped to advance Korean culture in Iran. The chapter also highlights the intertwined threads of all politico-economic and cultural elements which have played a rather invisible albeit indubitable role in the promotion and success of Hallyu among a fairly significant number of ordinary Iranian citizens, particularly over the past decade. In the final section, the chapter debates recent backlashes among some influential Iranians over the growing presence of Hallyu products in their society, in order to size up the prospects of Korean culture in Iran in the wake of a potential reintegration of the Persian Gulf country into the international system.

CHAPTER 1. INCOMPATIBLE YET INUNDATED: DIPLOMATIC, POLITICAL, AND MILITARY LINKS

The Classical Connections

Despite various attempts by Koreans, in ancient and recent times, to trace back their origin to the legendary Tangun or Dangun Wanggeom, who allegedly established the Korean kingdom of Gojoseon (Ancient Joseon) in 2333 B.C.,[1] there is really very little known, if anything at all, about the roots of the Korean nation. In the same way, there is also very little consensus among experts of various academic disciplines with regard to the early ancestors of the Japanese and Chinese people, as if the very genesis of the yellow race is destined to be shrouded in secrecy forever. Whether or not they originally came from North Africa or any other part of the greater Middle East region, in the form of a single tribe or separate tribes, they are widely thought to have crossed Central Asia, conventionally a heartland of the Iranian ancient empires, before arriving in their present locations in Northeast Asia, though widespread interbreeding, no matter whether voluntarily or arbitrarily, between these nations and other migrated people from the Pacific

---

1 As the mythical ancestor of the Korean nation, Tangun himself was a hybrid child born from the son of the emperor of heaven, Hwanung, and a female bear who was transformed into a woman. According to *Samguk Yusa* (Legends and History of the Three Kingdoms), Hwanung had descended to earth on the top of Mt. Taebaek (or presumably Mount Paektu or Baekdusan which is the highest mountain on the Korean Peninsula, straddling the present border between North Korea and China).

and Southeast Asian regions subsequently played an import role in shaping their overall national characteristics during the course of history.[2]

To some extent, a similar vagueness also exists about the terminology which has long been used, particularly by outsiders, to designate these nations as well as their languages. Iranians probably played an instrumental role in coining a number of terms applied to China and especially Korea. In older days, Iranians referred to the Goryeo dynasty as Koryo, long before the term was translated into Cauli in Italian, Corea in French, and Korea in English. After all, a magnum opus written (c. 846) by the Iranian historian and geographer Abulqasim Ibn Khordadbeh, *Kitab al-Masalik va al-Mamalik* (The Book of Roads and Kingdoms), turned out to be the first non-Asian reference to Korea available in recorded history.[3] One other influential source is the Persian epic poem *Kushnameh*, which provides a good reference to the ancient Silla.[4] The work is particularly well-known among Koreans, including former president Park Geun-hye, for depicting a supposedly romantic tale between a Persian prince and a Korean princess from the kingdom of Silla.[5]

There happened, therefore, to be miscellaneous connections between Iranian and Korean people in ancient times. Such interactions, directly and sometimes indirectly, were made possible primarily through the famous Silk Road, with the Chinese playing the role of an important intermediary between them.[6] Through these varied interchanges, Iranians are thought to have considerably influenced some material and non-material affairs of Koreans, ranging from arts and architecture to religion and reverential conviction.[7] A number of significant studies have shown how the bureaucratic

---

2   F.C. Jones, *The Far East: A Concise History* (London: Pergamon Press, 1966), pp. 34–36.

3 Frank Gosfield and Bernhardt J. Hurwood, *Korea: Land of the 38th Parallel* (New York: Parents' Magazine Press, 1969), p. 31.

4 "Hangug-uiilan, 1300 nyeon-ui inyeon," [Korea and Iran, Special Relations over 1,300 Years] *Yonhap News Agency*, September 28, 2016.

5 "Kushnameh; a Cultural Bridge Linking Iran, Korea," *Iran Book News Agency (IBNA)*, October 5, 2013; and "Pak daetongryeong 'yennal, pereusiawangjawa silla gongjuga saranghaesseoyo'," [President Parks Talks of 'Romance between Persian Prince and Silla Princess in Ancient Times'] *Seoul Shinmun*, May 3, 2016.

6 William Elliot Griffis, *Corea, Without and Within: Chapters on Corean History, Manners and Religion* (Presbyterian Board of Publication, 1885), pp. 252–254; and John Onians, *Atlas of World Art* (Oxford University Press, 2004), p. 141.

7 Hollym International Corporation, *Cultural Treasures of Korea: National Treasures 2: Ancient Tomb Relics, Ceramics, Handicraft Arts* (Seoul: Hollym International Corporation, 1993), p. 243.

system of the Sassanian Empire in ancient Persia may have influenced the Korean bureaucracy, and to some extent its Yangban mentality, during the Koryo and early Choson periods.[8] The Tang dynasty of China was especial-ly helpful in such contribution because under the Tang rule, the transfer of Iranian civilizational achievements to the East experienced its halcyon days, though part of this conveyance took place under certain unfortunate circum-stances that befell what was, at the time, Persia.

But Koreans not only borrowed from the Iranian legacy; they also became a transmitter of that heritage to their neighboring nations, the Japanese in particular. Because of its unique location, the Korean Peninsula was inexo-rably destined to be a bridge of sorts to transfer to the Japanese archipelago everything imaginable; from migrating people to manufactured products, and from loaned ideas to lullaby illusions.[9] Of course, such an intermediary role was not always played directly and voluntarily. Nor were the very acts of transferring goods and ideas from one part to another done immediately and perpetually. During the reign of the Mongols, for instance, the Korean Pen-insula itself became a hotbed of international interactions between people of various races and cultures. The Mongol-led elephantine bureaucracy had to increasingly rely on capable and qualified people from many other nations, such as Iranians, to manage its domestic and foreign affairs.[10] Even when the Mongols were eventually kicked out of the Korean Peninsula and China in total, the legacy and impact of previous interchanges over centuries did not swiftly disappear, even if direct people-to-people connections were largely interrupted for a couple of centuries to come.[11]

Perhaps nothing could epitomize such a perpetual influence more than the national flag of the modern Korean state; *Taegukgi*. In fact, the red and blue circle in the center of *Taegukgi* originally comes from the concept of good and evil forces taught by the ancient Iranian creeds of Zoroastrianism and

8 For instance, see: Mike Mason, *Global Shift: Asia, Africa, and Latin America, 1945–2007* (Montreal & Kingston: McGill-Queen's University Press, 2013), p. 110; and John B. Duncan, *The Origins of the Choson Dynasty* (Seattle, WA: The University of Washington Press, 2014), pp. 279–280.
9 Ernest F. Fenollosa, *Epochs of Chinese and Japanese Art: An Outline History of East Asiatic Design* (Berkeley, CA: Stone Bridge Press, 2007), p. 61.
10 George Lane, *Early Mongol Rule in Thirteenth-Century Iran: A Persian Renaissance* (London and New York: RoutledgeCurzon, 2003), pp. 223–225; and David M. Robinson, *Empire's Twilight: Northeast Asia under the Mongols* (Cambridge, MA: The Harvard University Asia Center, 2009), p. 52.
11 "Iran's Rich Art Heritage on Show in Korea," *Korea Times*, January 10, 2016.

Manichaeism. The four black trigrams on the *Taegukgi* likewise originate from the four classical elements (air, earth, fire, and water) developed initially by ancient Iranian scientists and thinkers, such as the renowned alchemist Jabir ibn Hayyan. However Koreans, like many of their peers in China, adamantly insist that the blue and red circle stems from the Chinese notion *yin* and *yang* (darkness and light), while *Taegukgi's* four black trigrams are also essentially a twisted version of the Chinese *wu xing* (the five changes or five phases). But the scope and extent of transformation and distortion wrought upon the Iranian legacy in the East, like some other parts of the world, is too complex and contentious to be succinctly explained here.[12]

Landing On Terra Nova: Modern Korea Discovers Iran

When the members of the first Korean goodwill mission arrived in Iran in 1957, they actually knew very little about the country or, for that matter, the complexity of the greater Middle East region. Various political issues seemed to baffle these newcomers, while confusing cultural matters were no easier to grasp. However, since the Koreans had already earmarked Iran as the most pivotal state in the region, strategically and politically, as well as a major land of economic opportunity, they were hell-bent on establishing official diplomatic ties at the earliest possible time.[13] Coming from a poor country recently devastated by a three-year-long fratricidal war and further shattered by interminable political instability and the dire economic situation of its citizens, they approached Iran with a big agenda of political and economic objectives without presenting even basic inducements to persuade their host country about those goals. When Seoul and Tehran eventually agreed to formally establish diplomatic relations in October 1962, more direct political contacts and closer interactions between the two sides had to wait for some time to come.

Part of the problem was that the Koreans had little to offer to most of their foreign counterparts, including the Iranians, to entice to forge closer ties. In addition to their backward economic circumstances domestically,

12 "'Glory of Persia' Shows Ancient Links Between Iran and Korea," *The Circle of Ancient Iranian Studies (CAIS)*, April 24, 2008; "Divar Gorgan kohantar az divar chin," [Gorgan Wall Older than Chinese Wall] *Tabnak*, May 29, 2010; and "Iranian Literature Showcased in Seoul," *Korea Herald*, January 11, 2016.
13 Ministry of Foreign Affairs, Republic of Korea, *Wegyo Munseo* [Diplomatic Archives] (Seoul: Republic of Korea, Ministry of Foreign Affairs, 1994).

the Korean officials had to jump through hoops and hurdles externally to convince other nations that they were the true leaders and legitimate representatives of all Koreans. Even when the Koreans commenced in earnest their industrialization and economic development programs in the early 1960s, they needed time to prove themselves on the international scene.[14] Another hurdle was that countries like Iran had very little vested interest in the Korean Peninsula, and thus they had little objective incentive to get involved. For instance, Tehran seemed to be more in favor of improving political and economic relations with Japan. Even the Republic of China (Taiwan) surprisingly rated better than the ROK; they were able to set up diplomatic ties earlier and politico-economic connections ensued between Tehran and Taipei.

But after scoring some economic progress at home, alliance politics conveniently made it possible for Seoul to swiftly push for political and economic interactions with a rather large number of like-minded political capitals such as Tehran from the early 1970s onward.[15] As a member of the anti-communist and pro-Western circle in which Iran had reserved a place, the ROK could benefit from such alliance advantages for both political and economic objectives which the East Asian country was adamantly seeking to achieve. The overall pattern of Iranian foreign policy often encouraged Tehran to throw its support behind Seoul in various Korea-related matters in the international arena, even when the issue at hand did not look entirely promising to Iranian officials. In the same way, the rather West-leaning diplomatic orientation of Iran had long facilitated some sort of close interactions between Tehran and the states of Japan and Taiwan, while such a political approach had forced the Iranian policymakers to distance their country from East Asia's communist countries of China and the Democratic People's Republic of Korea.

Long before Koreans managed to consolidate their interests in Iran in the 1970s, they started to discover the nuts and bolts about the Persian Gulf country soon after they opened an embassy and dispatched an ambassador

14 Henry S. Rowen, ed., *Behind East Asian Growth: The Political and Social Foundations of Prosperity* (London and New York: Routledge, 1998).
15 Ministry of Foreign Affairs, Republic of Korea, *Daehan minguk wegyo yeonpyo* [Republic of Korea, Annual Report on Foreign Policy] (Seoul: Ministry of Foreign Affairs, 1970), p. 279–281.

to reside in Tehran in April 1967. The documents declassified by the South Korean foreign ministry reveal that the Korean embassy in Tehran was even reporting to Seoul the volume and price of certain agricultural products in Iran, providing the relevant officials in the ROK with details on how the country could better serve their interests in various areas.[16] On top of that, the Tehran mission had become a major diplomatic post allowing Koreans to survey a greater number of countries in the Middle East by taking advantage of Iran's convenient location and considerable influence in the region.[17] At the same time, they could also keep a close eye on their Chinese and North Korean communist rivals in the Mideast, while learning timely and immutable lessons by observing various policies and strategies successfully implemented by their Japanese and Taiwanese allies in Iran and its neighboring territories.

Such a rather favorable environment for the ROK in Tehran changed slightly as Iran moved to ditch Taiwan in favor of mainland China and accepted negotiations with North Koreans, angering Seoul by ignoring its official request not to do so. However, the South Koreans could not keep their communist rivals at bay in Iran forever, nor were the Iranians willing to over-extend themselves in their alliance commitments. Pyongyang ultimately achieved its long-held desire to establish official diplomatic ties with Tehran in April 1973 and dispatched an ambassador to the Iranian capital right off the bat.[18] Although the North Koreans were jealous about the growing interests of their South Korean counterparts in Iran under the Pahlavi dynasty, nevertheless the Persian Gulf country was so attractive and promising to them that they were quite willing to cast aside, for now, their political and ideological proclivities in favor of making some well-meaning gestures toward the Iranians, as if they just knew that their own goods days in Iran were in the offing.[19]

---

16 *Wegyo Munseo* [Diplomatic Archives], 2001.
17 "Iranian Envoy Cited," *Korea Times*, April 26, 1972, p. 1.
18 "Taghirate jadid dar siyasate kharejiye Iran," ["New Changes in Iran's Foreign Policy"] *Ettelaat*, January 22, 1973; and "Ijad sefaratkhaneh koreye shomali dar Tehran," ["North Korean Embassy Established in Tehran"] *Ettelaat*, July 1, 1973.
19 Shirzad Azad, "Iran and the Two Koreas: A Peculiar Pattern of Foreign Policy," *The Journal of East Asian Affairs*, Vol. 26, No. 2 (2012), pp. 163–192.

Switching Allegiance: The Post-Pahlavi Era

In the aftermath of the political earthquake that toppled the Pahlavi dynasty and led to the establishment of the Islamic Republic in early 1979, Iranian foreign policy underwent seismic changes. The erstwhile pro-Western approach was replaced by a rather hostile attitude toward Western countries, the United States in particular, while Tehran's new orientation toward the broader international system significantly shifted in favor of self-reliance and anti-hegemonic proclivities.

Regional priorities in the Persian Gulf country's external affairs were systematically reconsidered, and in each region certain countries found a better chance to get closer to Iran. Although the new Iranian approach did not show much agitation with regard to East Asian countries, nevertheless, a fresh outlook gradually took hold and re-shaped the country's orientation toward the outside world. A part of the shift was to soon appear in Iran's relationship with the ROK, as Tehran had its own reasons not to fully succumb to new overtures from Seoul, seeking to keep the previous connections between the two countries intact.[20]

First and foremost, the political convulsions in Iran had threatened the stability experienced in political and economic relations between Seoul and Tehran over the course of more than one and half decades prior to the collapse of the Pahlavi monarchy. Despite its obsession with the West and desire for closer interactions with many non-Asian countries, the Pahlavi system had provided a rather conducive environment for Koreans to promote their growing interests in Iran. They could easily win many construction contracts, buy from Tehran as much as oil they wished, and ship to Iran's bustling markets a significant volume of Korean manufactured products. This established a productive trade relationship with Iran as compared to almost any other country in the Persian Gulf region. That is why the top Korean officials in Seoul, including the president, were in a hurry to express their willingness to the authorities in the Islamic Republic to at least maintain the previous relationship between the two countries. But regardless of the ROK's foreign policy approach, new allegations emerged against Seoul which could further undermine its teetering position in the Persian Gulf country.[21]

20 "Evacuation from Iran Expedited," *Korea Times*, February 4, 1979, p. 1.
21 "ROK–Iran Ties Desired to Remain Unchanged," *Korea Times*, January 18, 1979, p. 1.

South Korea was accused of having engaged in espionage activities in Tehran in favor of the United States in the aftermath of the so-called "hostage crisis" which led to the seizure of American diplomats for 444 days. Given the security alliance and long close cooperation between the ROK and the United States, there was no doubt that Seoul had quietly been rooting for the Americans and their interests in Iran, even when such accusations could not easily be proven. What made matters worse was that the Koreans were also charged with a more damning allegation, namely, that they had logistically cooperated with the United States during the botched operation masterminded by the US administration in Washington to rescue its diplomats held in Tehran.[22] With incriminating accusations of such genre, South Koreans could hardly appear more evil in the eyes of the new Iranian officials, but all they could do was to vehemently repudiate the charges and thoroughly dismiss their direct involvement in any wrongdoing against the Iranians.[23] South Korea's troubles over such allegations in Iran were, however, to supply grist for the mills of those who had been the main agents behind such leaks: the North Koreans.

The ascendancy of the Islamic Republic in Iran astonished the DPRK regime in Pyongyang; it was just a bolt from the blue. As a matter of fact, North Korea had striven for years to develop better connections in the wider Middle East region, but it had scarcely managed to get beyond a few socialist countries such as Egypt and Iraq. All Pyongyang could actually reap from these incessant endeavors in the region was some lukewarm political support and lackadaisical economic exchange. In the Persian Gulf, the DPRK had managed to establish official political ties with Iran and made economic inroads into a few Arab states such as Kuwait. But none of such rudimentary approaches and their meager achievements could really match what North Korea was to gain from a new, better relationship with Iran from 1979 onward. To the surprise of many, this new chapter in Pyongyang's relations with Tehran was to unfold in spite of a fierce anti-communism ide-

---

22 "Canada's Man in Tehran Was a CIA Spy," *The Globe and Mail*, January 23, 2010.
23 "Alleged ROK–U.S. Collusion: N.K. Iran Slur 'Unfounded'," *Korea Herald*, October 16, 1980, p. 1; "Seoul's Deputy Foreign Minister to Travel to Iran for Release of S. Korean National: Source," *Yonhap News Agency*, November 17, 2013; "Iran Releases Korean Jailed for Espionage," *Chosun Ilbo*, April 14, 2014; and "S. Korean Jailed for Spying in Iran Released," *Yonhap News Agency*, April 23, 2014.

ology embraced by a considerable number of new top officials of the Islamic Republic.[24]

The communist ideology, therefore, turned out not to be a major hurdle to closer political, and later military, relations between North Korea and Iran. There were some other political and ideological commonalities, and by capitalizing on those, North Korean and Iranian officials could cement the foundations of a robust relationship for a couple of decades to come. Pyongyang and Tehran had a somewhat similar view toward the international system; this attitude evolved primarily based on the vested interests of great powers. Additionally, North Korea could further improve its recent status in Tehran by denouncing various policies and actions of some pro-Western states, such as South Korea, so that the Iranian officials would have no serious doubt about the candidness and sincerity of Pyongyang's diplomats in Tehran.

Still, what really confirmed this new day for DPRK–Iran ties was the upcoming military conflict in the Persian Gulf which in an incredible way left Iranian officials dependent on communist North Korea for weapons supplies.[25]

The War And Its Spoils For Both Koreas

As the longest military conflict of the 20th century, the Iran–Iraq War (1980–1988) created an arms bonanza worth hundreds of billions of dollars. Great powers were major beneficiaries of this colossal windfall, but the armaments bazaar was commodious and lavish enough to embrace merchants of munitions from almost every part of the world. A good number of the arms dealers, including some who were really tenderfoots in the business, did not even bother to find out which party was actually right or wrong; they only cared to sell their weapons and charge handsomely. Many companies and individuals in the private sector, in addition to various rapacious states, were tempted to enter the bustling market and made a mint.

With regard to East Asian countries, the role of private merchants was minimal, but still the states often needed to resort to secretive tactics in order to ship their weapons to the warring parties in the Persian Gulf. The

---

24 Azad.
25 Azad.

two Koreas, North Korea in particular, were to greatly benefit from direct and indirect methods of arms supply to Tehran and Baghdad at one point or another during the course of the Iran–Iraq War.

North Korea's arms supply to Iran was so critical that it immediately led to the termination of diplomatic ties between Baghdad and North Korea, though the DPRK became so fascinated with the prospects of a burgeoning arms business with Iran that it did not care much about its ruptured relationship with Iraq. The arms deals with Iran promised to be so lucrative that the communist Koreans were ready to blithely forgo any more potential gain from a relationship with Iraq, whether in the political, military, or economic areas.[26] The Iran–Iraq War was in fact heaven sent for a cash-strapped state like North Korea, and Pyongyang wasted no time in replying positively when Iranian officials requested an arms shipment to Tehran.[27] Regardless of the overall size and value of North Korea's arms sales to Iran over the course of the military conflict, the deals entailed certain other perks for the DPRK. This relationship both improved and vouchsafed Pyongyang's political position in Tehran, so that Iran ultimately emerged as the communist state's most important partner in the entire Middle East region.

Moreover, the arms issue practically made the Chinese dependent on North Korea for their military deals with Tehran in the early years of the Iran–Iraq War. Unlike Pyongyang, Beijing was not really in a position to easily and comfortably engage directly in supplying weapons to Iran, once the military conflict broke out in September 1980. Big powers like China absolutely needed deniability in order to both save face and protect their larger politico-economic interests. China's communist comrades in the DPRK

---

26 "North Korea Said to Be Arming Iran," *New York Times*, December 19, 1982, p. 1.

27 In his memoirs, Akbar Hashemi Rafsanjani, who was one of the principal architects of Iran's military cooperation and arms deals with North Korea during the bloody wartime period, recalls part of the trip by his entourage to Pyongyang in September 1981 as follows "We also first visited the exhibition of agricultural machineries, and then went to see the University of Economics. They train the cadres, and all officials gather there one month every year to read the new discovered materials. They had made a replica for any type of exercise. The speaker of parliament (of North Korea) accompanied us wherever we visited, while he was simultaneously preaching against the United States and South Korea in favor of North Korea, Kim Il-sung, and the Communist Party. Later, we visited military bases to observe howitzer firing and to have a look at the North Korea-made tanks. We are planning to purchase a number of them. For the sake of the war, this is one of the important objectives of the trip." Cited from: "'Mehman marmooz' marasem tahlif ke bood," [Who was the 'Mysterious Guest' of Inauguration Ceremony] *Iranian Students' News Agency (ISNA)*, August 6, 2017.

could, therefore, give a hand by serving as a conduit for Beijing's arms deals with Tehran.

North Korea could have played a similar intermediary role for the Soviet Union's arms shipments to Iran. But unlike the Chinese case, there was very little, if any, hue and cry about Pyongyang facilitating some of Moscow's arms deals with Iran during the war. On top of that, North Korea's overall arms connections to Iran received lots of attention and agitation as compared to some other countries like South Korea.[28]

The ROK was essentially a second-tier arms merchant, as Seoul still had a long way to go before becoming a successful supplier in the market of armaments. South Korea was pretty much unknown at that time for any major achievement in other economic and technological areas, giving it little chance of soon emerging as a major partner in the arms market. But unlike their North Korean brethren, the South Koreans did not exclusively commit themselves to either Iran or Iraq. Neutrality toward the two warring parties was the official position of the ROK during the Iran–Iraq War, but such an ambiguous stance and the ensuing diplomatic bafflegab could also give Seoul a better chance to simultaneously deal with the governments in both Tehran and Baghdad.[29] After all, the international environment was relatively propitious for the ROK, enhancing its opportunities to engage in military dealings with either Iran or Iraq and then walk away relatively unscathed. The ROK's ace in the hole was that they had the blessing of the Americans, allegedly in part because the South Koreans were involved in some of Washington's own arms deals during the Iran–Iraq War.

In the infamous Iran–Contra scandal, the ROK all of a sudden became the subject of criminal investigations over its alleged role in the arms shipments. Rather than being questioned for breaking international sanctions laws, South Korea came under scrutiny primarily for assisting the Americans in peddling some of their sensitive military equipment in the Persian Gulf region. It was reported that an important role played by the ROK had been to supply US arms to the Persian Gulf using its commercial vessels.[30] Still, the entire scandal soon fizzled out and was consigned to historical archives.

28 Azad.
29 "Korea Impartial on Iran–Iraq War," *Korea Herald*, October 1, 1980, p. 1.
30 "U.S. Ambassador to South Korea under Scrutiny of Iran–Contra Probe," *Associated Press*, July 31, 1991.

The bold-faced people involved in the criminal case survived with impunity. Moreover, few details were known about whether or not the ROK had been assisted by experts from the private sector from one country or another in its work as a go-between.

Rekindling The Ties That Barely Bind

Although the South Koreans had demonstrated their intention to mend fences with the Iranians on a number of occasions over the course of the Iran–Iraq War, they became more stubborn and persistent about such matters when the conclusion of the military conflict between the Persian Gulf countries was in the offing. Of course, Seoul and Tehran had not terminated their diplomatic relationship entirely, but political ties between the two parties had sunk to the lowest level, as they were managing their connections through *chargés d'affaires* throughout the war period.

Since the end of war could herald new opportunities for Korean companies in the region, the Korean government had to lay the political groundwork for such an eventuality. Several rounds of negotiation led to an enhancement in diplomatic ties between South Korea and Iran so that the two countries could once again manage their official relations through the dispatch of a plenipotentiary ambassador. Contrary to all expectations, however, a real rapprochement between Seoul and Tehran was not to take place any time soon, because such a development was contingent upon a major shift in the relationship between the Western countries, the United States in particular, and Iran.[31]

The ROK's security agenda and its foreign policy priorities had long been tightly tied to those of the United States, keeping Seoul from rushing headlong and embracing post-war Iran wholeheartedly. Even South Korea's obsession with forging a better political relationship with Iran was not really just for the sake of closer political interactions but were meant to, first and foremost, smooth the way for accelerated economic relations between the two sides. On top of that, leading political and diplomatic officials of the two countries had sharply contrasting views with regard to a host of hot-button regional and international issues. Because of this hurdle, they would have agreed on very little even if they had had more opportunities to interact.

31 "Persian Gulf Crisis," *Korea Times*, September 25, 1980, p. 2.

Aside from the US factor, South Korea was also queasy about its vested interests in the greater Middle East region, as the East Asian country did not wish to harm those growing economic opportunities, partly or wholly, by appearing to be too close with Tehran diplomatically and politically.

In the Middle East, South Korea's perspective on the international situation was in fact considerably closer to that of many Arab states, such as Egypt, and especially member countries of the Gulf Cooperation Council (GCC). All of them were by and large in favor of a kind of alliance politics, whose main preferences and directions had been carved out largely by the United States. Stakes became even higher for South Korea when Seoul moved to enhance its diplomatic and political relations with Israel. In a political climate of distinct boundaries between Iran and many of its neighbors in the Middle East, therefore, the South Koreans had relatively little trouble in recognizing which party to side with. But since they had a vested interest in Iran, they could not easily engage in overt political disagreement, let alone a political dust-up, with Iran.[32] By keeping its political connections to Tehran subterranean, therefore, the ROK could handle its alliance commitments without harming its increasing economic interests in Iran; a strategy that neatly dovetailed with a similar policy promoted by Iran.

Basically, the end of the Iran–Iraq War and the commencement of the reconstruction era that followed did not really make pivotal changes in the Islamic Republic's prevailing approach toward the outside world. Hard politics and ideological proclivities were again to play a significant role in the country's interactions with many other nations. These core components did not disappear even when the Cold War came to an abrupt conclusion and Iran's overall relationship with former communist countries, Russia in particular, changed for the better. One major reason was that Iran had to keep carving out its external policies in terms of national-security-first, and politics-first, partly because the international system was behaving that way toward the Persian Gulf country. The politics-first approach was certainly more relevant in Iran's relationship with Western nations, but it also showed in Tehran's efforts to improve its ties with other parts of the world, East Asian states in particular, even when it needed to turn to them to meet its economic and technological requirements.

---

32 "Korean Workers Safe in Iran, Consul Says," *Korea Times*, January 6, 1979, p. 1.

In East Asia, for instance, Iran put more emphasis on its political and military connections to China and North Korea, while its politico-economic relationship with South Korea ultimately had to follow a trajectory roughly similar to that favored between Iran and Japan. The Tehran–Tokyo nexus was to serve as a role model for preserving bilateral relations between Tehran and Seoul in all political, economic, and even cultural areas. Iran had long been courting Japan for varied economic and technological services, but it had to pay only lip service to fostering robust political interactions with a country that was tightly enmeshed in political and security commitments involving the United States. Moreover, Japan was still in a position to bargain with the Americans over maintaining a semblance of political relations with Tehran without causing any serious damage to its alliance with Washington. If South Koreans could successfully emulate their Japanese counterparts on this matter, therefore, the lack of close political interactions would not really prevent Tehran and Seoul from persistently preserving, and even enhancing, their relationship in other areas.[33]

Vowing To Move Forward: Putting A Spotlight On Tehran–Pyongyang Ties

After diplomatic relations were established between Tehran and Pyongyang and in the final years of the Pahlavi dynasty, Iran managed its North Korean affairs through its embassy in Beijing, no matter if the DPRK had already set up its own embassy in the Iranian capital and dispatched an ambassador to manage its diplomatic mission there. Under the Islamic Republic, however, enhanced ties between the two sides encouraged Tehran to quickly and directly handle its North Korean affairs by dispatching a plenipotentiary ambassador to Pyongyang.

This was in sharp contrast to Iran's relationship with South Korea. During the Iran–Iraq War, good political ties between Iran and North Korea helped both countries to fully take advantage of their high-level political envoys in order to sort out various issues related to their military dealings. Embassies were a convenient place to manage serious bilateral talks over

---

33 "Top S. Korean, Iranian Diplomats Discuss Closer Ties," *Yonhap News Agency*, September 27, 2014; "Top S. Korean Official Due in Iran, Turkey," *Korea Herald*, June 23, 2015; and "To Iran with Love: The Political Nostalgia behind the South Korean President's Visit," *Policy Forum*, June 3, 2016.

many matters, ranging from political and military bargaining to economic and cultural exchanges. The end of the war was only to accentuate this crucial role of the Iranian and North Korean embassies in Pyongyang and Tehran, respectively.[34]

Meanwhile, the conclusion of the Iran–Iran War provided new grounds for cooperation between Iran and the DPRK. Both sides pledged to keep their war-time connections intact and even develop them into new areas. Besides maintaining friendly political ties, they aimed to especially ratchet up their joint activities in certain economic fields and sensitive military domains.

The war-time experiences had taught Iran to pay more attention to its defensive capabilities by investing in a number of critical military spheres, such as missile technology.[35] The DPRK was not really famous for being an advanced country in this respect, but it still could share with Iran some of its achievements in addition to maintaining cooperation with Tehran in conventional military sectors.[36] And unlike the war-time period when Pyongyang was in a position to hold an upper hand in its relationship with Tehran, this time certain circumstances at home and abroad could push, and even

---

34 "Taghdir safir koreye shomali dar Tehran az mavaze Iran," [North Korean Ambassador in Tehran Appreciates Iran Positions] *Asr Iran*, November 10, 2014; and "Tamjid vazir kharejeh koreye shomali az mardom Iran," [North Korean Foreign Minister Praises Iranian people] *Tabnak*, February 13, 2015.

35 In meeting with a visiting high ranking official of the Revolutionary Guards during the war period, the then North Korean top leader, Kim Il-sung, had apparently advised the Iranians to seek self-sufficiency in critical armaments and defense technologies by saying that "we sell you whatever we have, but why don't you go back to build such stuff in Iran." In order to better persuade the Iranians about the urgency of such a pivotal task, Kim had also narrated his own communist country's story: "In our battle with the Americans, the Eastern Bloc supported us. There was a certain division of labor, and each country was supposed to provide us with some help. Czechoslovakia, for instance, had been required to supply our bullets. One day, the country refused to give us bullets any longer. By predicting that the Czechoslovakian officials one day may stop sending us bullets, I had already built factories for making bullets but I had not informed them in advance about this development. The day Czechoslovakia refused to give us bullets, therefore, we had our own bullets to use. We also managed to use our own guns." Cited from: "Khoshhali 'Kim Il-sung' az sakht mooshak dar Iran: Tousiyeh jaleb rahbar vaght korye shomali be magham alirotbeh sepah," [Delight of 'Kim Il-sung' from Building Missile in Iran: Interesting Suggestion of the Then North Korean Leader to the High-ranking Official of the Revolutionary Guards] *Mizan Online News Agency*, March 31, 2017.

36 "Technology mooshaki Iran az korye shomali pishi gereft," [Iranian Missile Technology Outstripped North Korea] *Iranian Diplomacy*, December 15, 2012.

force, the DPRK leaders not to forgo any single opportunity in preserving and enhancing their connections to Iran.[37]

North Korea's economic hardship started roughly in the late 1970s, and the reclusive communist country's overall situation had not changed much for the better a decade later. As a matter of fact, pivotal changes in Russia and many Eastern European countries in the late 1980s and early 1990s had only made things worse, depriving Pyongyang of some of the economic and non-economic assistance it had been receiving from those nations since the late 1940s. North Korea was to suffer further troubles because of unfavorable climate conditions such as heavy rainfalls and droughts, making it difficult for the communist regime to support its citizens without asking reluctantly for help from the outside world.[38]

Moreover, an abrupt leadership transition in Pyongyang hurt the communist state's political and economic connections to a fair number of its friends and allies in different parts of the world. Such unwelcome and often detrimental domestic developments made Tehran a valuable and timely partner for Pyongyang, while new circumstances in East Asia, as well as in the Middle East, were to only push the two countries further toward serious engagement in all areas favorable to both sides.[39]

The disappearance of the Soviet Union from the Northeast Asian equation played right into the hands of Americans to further fortify their position in the region by stressing their security cooperation with Japan and South Korea. They also had to improve their political relationship with the Chinese, because the growing economic exchanges between the two great powers required them to titivate their ideological and geostrategic differences in favor of other vested interests very dear to each party. Even post-Soviet Russia was to be considered as an inevitable partner in the region, in order to

37 "Steinitz: Iran Deal Must Prevent Cooperation with North Korea," *Jerusalem Post*, November 21, 2014; "State: We Can't Deny Iran Nuclear Cooperation with North Korea; It Won't Stop Nuke Deal," *Washington Examiner*, May 28, 2015; and "Stop Iran by Stopping North Korea," *National Review*, October 22, 2016.
38 Marcus Noland, *Avoiding the Apocalypse: The Future of the Two Koreas* (Washington, DC: Institute for International Economics, 2000), pp. 89–91.
39 "Drought-hit North Korea Seeks Aid from Ally Iran," *The Daily Star*, June 30, 2015; "N.Korea Asks Iran for Drought Relief," *Chosun Ilbo*, July 3, 2015; and "North Korean Drought," *Korea Herald*, July 5, 2015.

play a constructive role in certain shared politico-diplomatic and economic interests.[40]

But to bring this coalition of odd partners together in East Asia, somebody had to play the role of bogeyman.[41] That is one reason why potential perils coming from the North Korean nuclear program were played up time and again, and Pyongyang's "suspicious relationship with Tehran" and its "negative ramifications" had to be noisily yet gratuitously put in the crosshairs of the world's mass media and public opinion.[42]

In the Middle East, and especially in the Persian Gulf region, the evaporation of the Cold War realities had likewise galvanized the United States into making unilateral maneuvers. Iraq's invasion of Kuwait and the ensuing military conflict were only to boost the physical presence and military might of the Americans in the region. They subsequently carved out the "dual containment" policy in order to add more pressure on both Iran and Iraq by denying them a range of economic and financial resources crucial to the post-conflict reconstruction in the two countries.

As a corollary to that, Iraq became more isolated and less powerful, but the Iranian situation was rather different.[43] It was neither possible to totally cut off Iran's connections to the outside world, nor could the United States harm the Persian Gulf country any further economically without going against some vital interests of Washington's friends and allies around the world. Still, to keep Iran in the penalty box, the Americans could at times play up Iran's relationship with some of its troublesome partners such as North Korea, but when the stakes became much higher, such "dubious connections" needed to be further accentuated; and that is what happened under the presidency of George W. Bush in Washington D.C.[44]

---

40 "Ravabet dirineh Tehran va Pyongyang," [Long-established Relations of Tehran and Pyongyang] *Rooz Online*, January 14, 2015.
41 Tim Beal, *North Korea: The Struggle against American Power* (London: Pluto Press, 2005), pp. 97–101.
42 "N. Korea Could Replace Iran as No. 1 Target of U.S. Nonproliferation Sanctions," *Yonhap News Agency*, July 21, 2015; and "Brookes: Iran, North Korea a Match Made in Nuke Heaven," *Boston Herald*, September 2, 2015.
43 Douglas Lemke, *Regions of War and Peace* (New York: Cambridge University Press, 2002), p. 63.
44 Robert E. Hunter, *Building Security in the Persian Gulf* (Santa Monica, CA: RAND, 2010), pp. 49–51.

The Fictitious Axis: Iran And North Korea Team Up

In the wake of the September 11th incident in the United Sates, the Bush-led US administration put North Korea along with Iraq and Iran on a dubious list tagged the "axis of evil." Iraq had long been a target of harsh US policies, and the personal animosity of the Bush family toward the Iraqi leader, Saddam Hussein, was an open secret, though there was still hardly any rationale for the DPRK to be in league with Iraq. But for most bona fide experts and long-term observers of US policies in both regions, there was really no reasonable justification to associate North Korea's rather isolationist foreign policy with those proactive policies followed by Iran as the *de facto* native hegemon of the Middle East region.[45] It was also the first time that Koreans and Iranians had arbitrarily been associated so loudly and so negatively throughout the world. The main objective was to give the foreign policy behaviors of the three countries a negative spin in world opinion, suggesting they were an imminent threat to the peace and prosperity of the world in order to ultimately rally as many independent states as possible in different parts of the world behind the hidden agenda of the Bush administration.[46]

The fanciful notion of the "axis of evil" was subsequently lectured to a larger number of people around the world through influential media as well as by prejudiced pundits active in both academic and policy circles.[47] Books were penned, reports were carved out, seminars were convened, and interviews were arranged through all of which particular emphasis was put on the North Korean–Iranian relationship and how such a nexus posed an existential threat to the United States and its allies and friends.[48] Moreover,

---

45 Robert J. Jackson and Philip Towle, *Temptations of Power: The United States in Global Politics after 9/11* (New York: Palgrave Macmillan, 2006), pp. 46–47.

46 Patrick M. Cronin (ed.), *Double Trouble: Iran and North Korea as Challenges to International Security* (Westport, CT: Praeger Security International, 2008).

47 "Iran Crisis Increasingly Tied to North Korea," *World Politics Review*, April 4, 2013; "Was the Iranian Threat Fabricated By Israel and the U.S.?" *Haaretz*, May 31, 2014; "U.S. to Probe Allegations that Iran, North Korea Are Linked in Nuclear and Missile Research," *Washington Times*, May 29, 2015; and "Is Iran Really So Evil?" *Politico Magazine*, January 17, 2016.

48 Wade L. Huntley, "Rebels without a Cause: North Korea, Iran and the NPT," *International Affairs*, Vol. 82, No. 4 (2006), pp. 723–742; "North Korea and Iran Increase Collaboration on Nuclear Missile, Report Claims," *Telegraph*, July 21, 2011; "Iran, North Korea as Proliferation Epicenters," *Asia Times*, June 3, 2014; "Iran's Partnership with North Korea on Nukes and Missiles May Scuttle Any Deal," *Forbes*, February 20, 2015; and "Iran, North Korea Forging Ballistic, Nuclear Ties: Dissidents," *Reuters*, May 28, 2015.

trade data and commercial statistics were sometimes twisted so that they could signify the size and scope of an imagined close partnership between Pyongyang and Tehran.[49]

Still, no aspect of relations between the DPRK and Iran was accentuated more than their cooperation on missile and nuclear energy technologies, though the Iranian government often boasted about its self-sufficiency, its ability to meet the country's requirements in those areas without any dependency on foreign partners such as North Korea.[50] But what really forced the United States to play up the potential perils of Pyongyang–Tehran ties in the first place?

By drawing attention to the Iranian–North Korean nexus, the Bush administration could partially assuage its growing troubles in both the Middle East and East Asia.[51] The US war in Afghanistan had failed to achieve its alleged, if fanciful, goal of "economic development and democracy promotion," while the Iraq War of 2003 was to take a further toll on America's international reputation, with no quick fix in the offing. The chaos and insurgency that ensued in Iraq drained more human and financial resources from the United States and its coalition partners. The psychological drama for the US government was no less pressing, since no weapons of mass destruction had been unearthed in Iraq, and skeptics no longer found it remotely plausible that Saddam was in any way connected to 9/11. To fight back, therefore, one strategy was to pin the blame on the Iranian government for its role behind the insurgency in Iraq. And to make this idea work better, it was necessary to widely underscore the expanding power of Iran by putting heavy empha-

---

49 "Iran Could Outsource Its Nuclear Program to North Korea," *Wall Street Journal*, June 20, 2014; "North Korea and Iran: Partners in Cyber Warfare?" *Forbes*, December 12, 2014; "Does Iran Have Secret Nukes in North Korea?" *Daily Beast*, March 29, 2015; and "North Korea Transfers Missile Goods to Iran during Nuclear Talks," *Washington Free Beacon*, April 15, 2015.

50 "Ahmadinejad: No Military Cooperation with DPRK," *Daily Yomiuri*, November 30, 2007; "Debunking the Iran–North Korea Nuclear Axis Myth," *The Diplomat*, April 23, 2014; "Middle East's Misery and South Korea–Japan Peace," *Donga*, February 12, 2015; "It's North Korea, all over again," *Washington Times*, June 29, 2015; and "Double Standard: N. Korea and Iran," *Toronto Star*, September 16, 2016.

51 "Iran Sees No Linkage to N. Korea's Nuke Program: Envoy," *Yonhap News Agency*, September 25, 2014; "Focus on North Korea to Stop Iran," *New York Post*, April 30, 2015; "Opinion: Iran as Munich in 1938, North Korea in 1994," *Los Angeles Times*, July 25, 2015; and "Iran's North Korea Loophole," *Commentary Magazine*, February 3, 2016.

sis on the Persian Gulf country's nuclear as well as missile programs and North Korea's assistances to Tehran in such areas.[52]

In East Asia, the United States was somewhat queasy about various pro-Pyongyang policies pursued by the so-called liberal and progressive governments of Kim Dae-jung (1998–2003) and Roh Moo-hyun (2003–2008) in South Korea. No matter whether the US administration was democrat or republican, both leaders were ultimately opposed to certain American policies toward the Korean Peninsula in general and the DPRK regime in particular. Even when the United States was mired in the Middle East in the wake of the Iraq War, Washington could not let the South Korean government fully engage the DPRK regime. But for the sake of its vested interests in East Asia, and especially the Korean Peninsula, neither could the United States openly and widely discredit the ROK's pro-Pyongyang policies. One safe and immediate remedy was, therefore, to highlight the danger of the North Korean nuclear program by drawing an analogy between the reverberations which supposedly were to stem from a "bellicose behavior" of the DPRK and the ongoing "pugnacious policies" of its Iranian partner in the Middle East.[53] But could such an ill-advised analogy really hold water at all?

North Korea was not in a strong position to threaten a well-armed South Korea, let alone Japan and the United States.[54] The nuclear and missile capabilities of the DPRK had long been grossly exaggerated, and the feeble communist state had little in the way of even conventional military, let alone newfangled armaments, as compared to other countries in East Asia. North Korea had been cornered for decades, and a slew of economic sanctions constantly levied against Pyongyang had badly hurt the foundations of its financial and military strength. The DPRK was usually in favor of seclusion, did not pursue recklessly adventurous policies abroad, and its occasional saber-rattling against South Korea was more about acquiring its immediate

---

52 "Iran–North Korea's 'Axis of Evil' Revived by New Nuclear Ties," *National Post*, March 14, 2013; "Iran–Syria–North Korea Nuclear Nexus," *FrontPage Magazine*, January 28, 2015; and "Does Iran Have Secret Nukes in North Korea?" *Daily Beast*, March 29, 2015.
53 Lemke, pp. 82–86.
54 "N. Korea Biggest Threat to US: Poll," *Korea Times*, January 17, 2017.

needs — denied by one or another sanctions policy in which Seoul was to be blamed as a culprit.[55]

In spite of such knotty, endemic problems, much was said and written about various imagined similarities between North Korea and Iran in order to give credence to the "axis of evil" delusion.[56] At the same time, when it came to the ever-expanding relationship between South Korea and Iran, particularly in the economic, financial, and technological fields, there was a lack of media coverage and a dearth of information.

In One Single Package: Muddling Through Sanctions

One peculiar characteristic of the Iranian–South Korean relationship under the presidency of Ahmadinejad was that a lack of good political ties coincided with a high-level economic turnover between the two countries.[57] In fact, political interactions among top officials of the two countries reached an all-time low since the conclusion of the Iran–Iraq War in late 1980s, while Seoul and Tehran surprisingly experienced the acme of their economic exchanges since they established their diplomatic ties in 1962.[58]

Although there happened to be irregular parliamentarian visits and an occasional dispatch of low-level diplomats and non-political envoys between Iran and the ROK, nonetheless, official contacts at higher levels ceased to exist almost for the entire period of Ahmadinejad's presidency.[59] Yet astonishingly, the two parties managed to enjoy an unprecedented level of economic

---

55 "The Iran–North Korea Axis of Atomic Weapons?" *Forbes*, August 13, 2015; and "The Iran–North Korea Connection," *The Diplomat*, April 20, 2016.

56 Alexander T.J. Lennon and Camille Eiss (eds.), *Reshaping Rogue States: Preemption, Regime Change, and U.S. Policy toward Iran, Iraq, and North Korea* (Cambridge, MA: The MIT Press, 2004).

57 "S. Korea Moving to Hold FM Talks with Iran in New York," *Yonhap News Agency*, September 22, 2014.

58 "Iran and South Korea Highlight Cooperation," *Tehran Times*, May 27, 2014; "Iranian, S. Korean Parliamentary Think Tanks Ink Cooperation Agreement," *Fars News Agency*, June 22, 2014; and "Foreign Minister to Visit Iran Saturday," *Korea Times*, November 3, 2015.

59 "South Korea's Parliament Speaker to Visit Iran for Talks," *Xinhua*, January 26, 2014; "Assembly Leader Returns to Seoul after Iran Trip," *Korea Times*, February 2, 2014; "Iran, South Korea Underline Widening Ties in Parliamentary Research," *Fars News Agency*, November 22, 2014; "Parl. Delegation Due in S. Korea," *Mehr News Agency*, June 6, 2015; and "N. Korea–Iran Nuclear Ties Probably Deep: Report," *Washington Times*, January 28, 2016.

and financial connections without much diplomatic and political fanfare going on between Tehran and Seoul.[60]

Still, the burgeoning economic relationship between Seoul and Tehran was fraught with its own anomalies as well. The ROK was toeing the line with regard to certain American political diktats against Iran, and the Koreans were also forced to participate in various economic punishments against Tehran according to one or another sanctions law.[61] Of course, South Korea was more cautious than Japan in terms of publicly denouncing Iranian policies, particularly those related to the nuclear controversy. Despite their considerable prudence, however, the ROK was not able to steer clear of all punitive economic measures levied against the Persian Gulf country. And the sanctions-related steps intended to hurt Iranian interests inevitably hurt the interests of Korean companies as well, sometimes severely. The ROK was adamant in pursuing its economic interests in Iran, and it was a major challenge to maintain the appearance of going along with the sanctions regime at the same time. How did they manage it? The answer can be partly found by comparing American, Korean, and Iranian policies.

The United States almost always talked to the ROK behind the scenes with regard to the political and economic measures which Washington had in mind against Iran. The Americans hardly ever made public their disagreements with South Korea, lest the appearance of a less-than-unified front further damage their so-called security alliance. Any potential dissension might be taken advantage of by a third party, especially the communist regime of the DPRK. And when South Koreans were pushed, *sotto voce*, by the United States to go along with certain sanctions policies against Iran, they were still allowed wiggle room to partially make up for the losses incurred by Korean companies. The ROK was particularly exempted on multiple occasions, when Washington produced a carefully cherry-picked list of countries which could go on doing business with Iran without negative consequenc-

---

60 "Safar Larijani be Seoul," [Larijani's Travel to Seoul] *Bultan News*, October 4, 2014; "Hangug wegyojanggwan 14nyeonman Iran pangmun...bukhane mesiji?" [South Korean Foreign Minister Visits Iran in 14 Years...Messages to North Korea?] *Yonhap News Agency*, November 7, 2015.

61 "Enhanced Sanctions Export Despair to Korea," *Korea Joongang Daily*, July 2, 2013; "Korean Businesses Hopeful as Iran Sanctions Ease," *Chosun Ilbo*, January 15, 2014; "S. Korean Firms Pin Hopes on Lifting of Iran Sanctions," *Korea Herald*, April 3, 2015; and "South Korea Credit Agency Pledges to Help Firms Snare Iran Business," *Reuters*, July 16, 2015.

es.[62] Such ad hoc permissions sometimes even enabled Korean companies to increase their market shares in Iran in the absence of foreign competitors.[63]

The South Korean government, whether liberal or conservative, also played a part in sorting out obvious differences with both Washington and Tehran about the Iranian nuclear controversy and the pertinent sanctions. The ROK might cooperate with the Americans in some other policy matters in order to get certain advantages from Washington with regard to its peculiar ties with Tehran.[64] By resorting to conventional diplomatic bafflegab, moreover, South Korea could occasionally agree with the United States only verbally, or on paper, without really committing itself to fully implementing whatever the Americans asked it to do.[65] On top of that, the South Koreans often used to ask their Iranian counterparts for forgiveness because they could not continue to resist the American arm-twisting. The ROK's top representatives in Tehran, or at international institutions such as the United Nations (UN), were one channel by which Seoul could let Tehran know that it was not going to be able to continue to withstand pressures from Washington and to ask for understanding and cooperation.[66]

For its part, the Iranian government could simply take it for granted that sustained American pressure on South Korea was real indeed; and this understanding obviated public censure by Iranian officials when the ROK took anti-Iran measures. And since Iran had sometimes been bludgeoned into restricting its international commerce to a certain number of states, and since few countries were in a position to readily replenish its technological

---

62 "U.S. to Renew Exemptions for Nations Importing Iran Oil," *Bloomberg*, June 5, 2013; "Green Light for Korea's Trade with Iran," *Business Korea*, January 22, 2014; "Japan, S. Korea to Maintain Iranian Crude Oil Import Volumes in 2014," *Tehran Times*, May 2, 2014; and "Iran Aims to Win Back Oil Sales to South Korea: Ambassador," *Tehran Times*, May 20, 2015.

63 "US Faces Sanctions Dilemma in East Asia," *Asia Times*, July 21, 2012; and "Iranian Sanctions Have Cost U.S. Economy Up to $175 Billion, Study Says," *Time*, July 14, 2014.

64 "Iran wonyu keumsujocheo, urido dongchamhaeya hana?" [Do We Need to Join Iran Oil Embargo?] *Hankyoreh*, January 10, 2012; "Hoshdar vazir naft Iran be koreye jenoobi," [Iran Oil Minister's Warning to South Korea] *Tabnak*, June 28, 2012; and "Didar safir koreye jenoobi dar Tehran ba Zarif," [South Korean Ambassador to Tehran Meets Zarif] *Tabnak*, November 7, 2015.

65 Harald Olsen, "South Korea's Pivot toward Iran: Resource Diplomacy and ROK–Iran Sanctions," *The Korean Journal of Defense Analysis*, Vol. 25, No. 1 (March 2013), pp. 73–85.

66 "Korea, Iran Seek Ministerial Talks at U.N.," *Korea Herald*, September 22, 2014; and "If Sanctions End, Korea Intends to Profit in Iran," *Korea Joongand Daily*, April 3, 2015.

and financial requirements, it could not run the risk of losing a major foreign partner such as South Korea by publicly denouncing their official position toward Iran-related policies. Such an approach could also backfire domestically, because it had the potential to lead policymakers and even ordinary citizens to question their country's overall engagement with South Korea in the wake of Seoul's blatant apparent willingness to harm them in one way or another.[67] After all, the Iranian predicament was not going to last forever, and once the unfavorable circumstances changed for good, the government would be in a far better position to manage its relationship with South Korea.[68]

On The Coattails Of The Nuclear Deal: The East–West Rivalry In Iran Heats Up

With the ascension of Hassan Rouhani to the Iranian presidency in August 2013, tackling the country's chronic and knotty foreign policy problems became a priority for the new government. Since Iran had suffered a major setback from the nuclear controversy under Ahmadinejad, none of the external issues facing the country mattered more than the daunting task of negotiating a peaceful resolution to the nuclear stalemate.[69]

After a long, drawn-out process of intensive negotiations over some 18 months, Iran and the 5+1 party (United States, Britain, France, Russia, China, and Germany) issued a document entitled the Joint Comprehensive Plan of Action (JCPOA) in June 2015, according to which Iran could be relieved of the international sanctions in exchange for scaling back in its nuclear program.[70]

---

67 "Kore pishgam tahrimhay gharb aleih Iran: Chera Iran dar moghabel kore skoot kardeh ast?" [Korea Prime Mover of Western Sanctions against Iran: Why is Iran Lapsed into Silence before Korea?] *Mashregh*, April 30, 2013; and "Kore bayad bimehri zaman tahrim ra jobran konad," [Korea Should Make up for Mischief in Sanctions Times] *Jahan News*, February 20, 2016.

68 "Tahrimhay yekjanebeh koreye jenoobi aleih Iran," [South Korea's Unilateral Sanctions against Iran] *Tabnak*, September 8, 2010.

69 Scott Sagan, Kenneth N. Waltz, and Richard K. Betts, "A Nuclear Iran: Promoting Stability or Courting Disaster?" *Journal of International Affairs*, Vol. 60, No. 2 (Spring 2007), pp. 135–150.

70 "The Iran Deal: The View from Asia," *Foreign Policy*, April 8, 2015; "Worried about Being Left out of Investment Bonanza, Japan Eyes Sending Foreign Minister to Iran," *Japan Times*, September 5, 2015; and "A Safer World, Thanks to the Iran Pact," *New York Times*, January 18, 2016, p. A20.

But the JCPOA was not only about a lasting settlement to the Iranian nuclear problem. The deal had long been predicted by impartial experts from all sides as a means to reintegrate the country into the international system, albeit gradually, bit by bit. Although the nuclear deal was a highly important factor in resolving some of Iran's crippling problems at home and abroad, it was equally critical for foreign countries which had long had pivotal interests in the country.[71]

Long before the nuclear deal was clinched, most of those concerned nations, eager to do business, were waiting in the wings to start their own bilateral negotiations with Iran in order to get back into the country's bustling markets.[72] For Western companies, the stakes were particularly high because they had been grudgingly forced to leave Iran, primarily over the nuclear controversy and the sanctions.[73] In their absence, new rivals had entered Iran's lucrative markets and increased their market shares.[74]

Still, among the Western countries, Europeans were more attentive to such developments and therefore were very enthusiastic to see a quick solution for the Iranian nuclear problem in the offing. Once Iran and its negotiating counterparts in the 5+1 party gave the thumbs up to the nuclear agreement, many member countries of the European Union (EU) dispatched high-profile politicians or delegates from the private sector to Tehran in order to at least recapture part of their previous business from rivals, especially from Asian countries such as China and South Korea.[75]

71 "Carmakers Eye Golden Iranian Opportunity in Wake of Nuclear Deal," *Financial Times*, July 15, 2015; "Britain in Danger of Losing the Race to Iran Before It's Begun," *Telegraph*, July 31, 2015; "South Korean Officials Visit Iran to Seek Post-sanction Deals," *Reuters*, August 22, 2015; and "Iran Welcomes 145 Delegations from 48 Countries in 9 Months," *Mehr News Agency*, January 2, 2016.

72 "S. Korea Congratulates Rowhani's Win in Iran Presidential Vote," *Yonhap News Agency*, June 18, 2013; "S. Korea Hails Iranian Nuclear Deal," *Yonhap News Agency*, July 14, 2015; and "S. Korea Expects Iranian Nuclear Deal to Affect N. Korea," *Yonhap News Agency*, July 9, 2015.

73 Robert S. Litwak, "Living with Ambiguity: Nuclear Deals with Iran and North Korea," *Survival: Global Politics and Strategy*, Vol. 50, No. 1 (2008), pp. 91–118.

74 A. Cooper Drury, *Economic Sanctions and Presidential Decisions: Models of Political Rationality* (New York: Palgrave Macmillan, 2005), pp. 11–12; and "US Threatens Sanctions over Shell Investment in Iran," *Financial Times*, November 15, 1999, p. 29.

75 "Business in Iran: Awaiting the Gold Rush," *The Economist*, November 1, 2014; "Czech Republic Prepares for Export Boom to Iran," *Radio Prague*, November 9, 2015; "Air France Announces New New York Route, Will Resume Iran Flights," *USA Today*, December 8, 2015; "The Eight Great Powers of 2016: Iran Joins the Club," *The American Interest*, January 26, 2016; and "The Emergence of Iran," *Business Standard*, May 24, 2016.

In spite of their alacrity and preparedness to go back to Iran, European countries could not simply rush into the embrace of the Iranians and engage headlong in any business whatsoever with them. They encountered a number of critical financial and technical issues, such as banking and trade regulations, which could significantly forestall any swift and robust economic and technological relationship with Iran.[76]

The United States was the culprit, putting up hurdles — some of which had nothing to do with the nuclear controversy.[77] The Europeans, therefore, had to first bargain with their American allies to convince them to lift at least some of those impediments before they could engage in full-fledged commercial relations with Iran.[78] There was no easy fix because a great part of the problem was contingent upon American domestic politics as well as the vested interests of its companies, some of which were equally, if not more, willing to tap into Iran's huge potential.

In the same way, almost all Eastern countries were striving to hold onto their opportunities in the new "gold rush" in Iran.[79] Particularly in East Asia, there happened to be two groups of stakeholders, excluding North Korea, whose obsessions about a fresh business bonanza in Iran differed markedly from each other. One group consisted of Japan and Taiwan, which were ruminating how to regain their lost market shares in the Persian Gulf country. Prior to the imposition of international sanctions over the nuclear problem, Japan and Taiwan used to import considerable energy resources from Iran and they would ship back to the country a significant amount of manufactured products. Taiwan and particularly Japan, however, had had to forgo most of their economic connections to Tehran in the wake of tightening

76 "SWIFT ra kheili gran dour mizadim," [We Were Bypassing SWIFT at High Cost] *Taadol*, December 5, 2015, p. 1; and "Iran Tries to End Its Isolation But So Much Stands in the Way," *Financial Times*, May 4, 2016.

77 "The Democrats Own Iran," *Wall Street Journal*, April 22, 2015; "How the Nuclear Deal will Fund Iran's Imperialism," *Washington Post*, August 3, 2015; "Hassan Rouhani: Republicans Couldn't Find Iran on A Map," *CNN*, September 28, 2015; "Iran Moves from Pariah State to Regional Power," *Reuters*, January 18, 2016; and "Iran Is Back in Business," *Financial Times*, January 29, 2016.

78 "In Tehran, Iranians Play Down Milestone," *New York Times*, January 16, 2016; and "A Year after the Nuclear Deal, Iranian Optimism Turns Sour," *Washington Post*, September 23, 2016.

79 "From Pariah to Powerhouse: The Iran Nuclear Deal and the New Land of Opportunity," *Forbes*, August 24, 2015; "Iran Is About to Become the Biggest Free-for-all since the Soviet Collapse," *Quartz*, June 25, 2015; and "IMF Official Says There's a 'Buzz' About Doing Business with Iran," *The Weekly Standard*, June 29, 2016.

sanctions.[80] Although both countries had been rewarded in various ways by the Americans for their political and economic cooperation on the Iranian nuclear issue, they were hell-bent on returning to Iran as soon as the international environment allowed such a move.[81]

The second group of East Asian countries included China and South Korea.[82] Unlike Tokyo and Taipei, Beijing and Seoul were concerned primarily with how to at least maintain their current strong positions in Iran, in case circumstances blocked them from actually revving up their market penetration. After all, both were major winners in the ruthless regime of sanctions against Iran, and their success had aroused the jealousy of their rivals in both the East and West. Unlike the ROK, the People's Republic of China (PRC) could raise some of these concerns with its partners in the 5+1 party during the nuclear negotiations. Moreover, Iranian officials had assured Beijing umpteen times that they had no plan to replace the Chinese companies with new business partners from other parts of the world once circumstances changed for better in Iran.[83] South Koreans were, therefore, very anxious to safeguard their pivotal interests in Iran when that country was moving confidently to mend fences with the West and consequently let into the country a horde of voracious new competitors from all over the world.[84]

In an interview with the Japanese *Nikkei*, Jaehong Kim, President of the state-run Korea Trade-Investment Promotion Agency (KOTRA), expressed such understanding and feeling clearly and succinctly by saying that "big

---

80 "Iran's Nuclear Deal Likely Boon to Korean Economy: KITA," *Korea Herald*, April 5, 2015; "New Chapter in Iran Ties with Three Continents," *Iran Daily*, November 7, 2015; and "Iran Deals will Spur Economy: Park," *Korea Times*, May 11, 2016.

81 "The Iran Nuclear Deal: As Seen From Asia," *The Diplomat*, November 26, 2013; "Iran Deal and Koreas," *Korea Times*, July 7, 2015; "Iran Nuke Deal Seen to Help Korean Firms Resume Biz Ties," *Yonhap News Agency*, July 14, 2015; and "Korea, Iran to Revive Economic Ties," *Korea Times*, January 26, 2016.

82 "Iran Nuke Deal Pleases Seoul," *Korea Joongang Daily*, April 4, 2015; "Iran Nuke Deal to Energize Trade with Korea," *Korea Herald*, May 19, 2015; "Iran's Opening Awaited by Korean Companies," *Korea Joongang Daily*, July 16, 2015; "Iranian Nuclear Deal Boon for Korean Builders," *Business Korea*, July 16, 2015; and "Korea to Benefit from Lifting of Iran Sanctions," *Korea Times*, January 17, 2016.

83 "'Bonjolhay chini' bazar ra be dast greftand," ['Chinese Gimcracks' Captured the Market] *Tabnak*, January 31, 2015; "From Buyers to Competitors: Korean Oil Companies' Exports to Middle East Facing Threat," *Business Korea*, March 31, 2015; and "Iran Opportunities 'Too Big to Ignore': CEO," *CNBC*, January 28, 2016.

84 "Iran's Trade with Europe, US Picks up," *Press TV*, February 26, 2015; "Iran Opens for Business," *New York Times*, January 18, 2016; "Iran's Dealmaking with Europe: The Seven Biggest Contracts," *Guardian*, January 29, 2016; and "Sign of Thaw with Iran: American Cellphones Ringing in Tehran," *New York Times*, October 8, 2016.

opportunities are coming to Iran, with markets that were once closed due to the sanctions opening up all at once."[85] In order to up the ante and achieve those critical objectives all at one fell swoop, the "CEO" of Korea Inc., President Park Geun-hye, soon conducted a watershed visit to the Persian Gulf country, though she did not survive in office long enough to reap all the benefits of her historic move.[86]

The Tie-Up Trip: Park Visits Tehran

Park Geun-hye became the first South Korean president to pay an official visit to Iran on May 1–4, 2016. Prior to that, no Korean top leader, not even from North Korea, had gone to Tehran.[87] In fact, such a crucial event had not taken place even during the reign of her father, Park Chung-hee, when the ROK and Iran enjoyed a more propitious environment in their bilateral political relations.

For an uninterrupted diplomatic relationship more than six decades old, therefore, great importance was attached to Park's tour to Tehran. Moreover, the South Korean president embarked upon this journey at a crucial time when the prospects were not clear for Iran's ongoing yet cautious interactions with influential Western countries.[88] Whether or not the United States had endorsed Park's visit, explicitly or implicitly, she most probably could not have planned such an event in the absence of a tacit agreement from the Obama administration. After all, the frosty environment in the ROK's political ties with Iran was largely due to Washington's policies toward Tehran during the past decades.[89]

That is one pivotal reason why so much was published and broadcast about the economic and cultural aspects of her Iran trip — in order to wa-

---

85 "S. Korea Trade Promotion Agency Sees Opportunities in Iran," *Tehran Times*, October 21, 2015.

86 "South Korean Prosecutors Seek 30 Years' Jail for Ousted Park as Supporters Demand Her Release," *New York Times*, February 27, 2018.

87 "In Diplomatic Flurry, Park Considers Iran Visit," *Korea Herald*, January 27, 2016; and "Park in Iran," *Korea Herald*, May 1, 2016.

88 "France Opens Trade Office in Iran," *New York Times*, September 21, 2015; "German Companies Hope for A Bonanza in Iran," *Deutsche Welle*, December 31, 2015; "France Welcomes Iran's President — and His Checkbook," *USA Today*, January 28, 2016; "Park Arrives in S. Korea after Groundbreaking Trip to Iran," *Yonhap News Agency*, May 4, 2016; and "EU Eyes Return as Iran's First Trade Partner," *Al-Monitor*, June 1, 2016.

89 "Pak daetongryeong, Iran sales wegyo sijak," [President Park Kicks off Sales Diplomacy with Iran] *Hankook Ilbo*, May 2, 2016.

ter down its political significance. To skillfully divert international atten-tions from the political element, Park's trip to Tehran was dubbed a matter of "economic diplomacy," "sales diplomacy," "cultural diplomacy," "Roosari diplomacy," and so on. Little if anything was said about the invisible US fac-tor in arranging and making possible such a politically sensitive official trip.

Although the Iranian nuclear deal had brought some crucial positive changes to Tehran's overall interactions with the outside world, still many close allies of the United States kept behaving extremely prudently in deal-ing with Iran. As a case in point, the Japanese Prime Minister, Shinzo Abe, later had to put his important scheduled official visit to Tehran on hold until after the US presidential elections in November 2016.[90]

Regardless of the US component adumbrated above, Park's Tehran ad-venture was critical for both the ROK and Iran politically, economically, and culturally. A key objective was to stir up enough enthusiasm and support to renew and expand the relationship between the two countries in the wake of the Iranian nuclear deal. The political message of the trip was crystal clear, while the economic weight of Park's entourage surprisingly was character-ized as "the largest business delegation in the history of Korean presidential trips" to a foreign country. The cultural ramifications were also significant as Park participated in some cultural events during her sojourn in Tehran, and a number of important cultural documents were signed between the two sides.[91] The plucky passion attached to the trip may be partially chalked up to the energetic press and media coverage in both countries which widely promoted all developments during her stay in Tehran, while concerned Ira-nian observers in the media and policy circles exercised self-restraint and abstained from criticizing the visiting South Koreans for various negative reverberations of their economic omnipresence in Iran.

Beyond Iran, moreover, Park's trip was intended to enhance South Ko-rea's foreign relations with the broader Middle East. By opening "new hori-zons in Korea's Middle East diplomacy," Park's achievements in Iran prom-ised to partially make up for her rather lackadaisical record in the region.[92]

90 "Abe Eyes Visiting Iran in August," *Kyodo News Agency*, April 6, 2016.
91 "Sales Diplomacy: 66 MOUs Signed at S. Korea–Iran Summit Meeting," *Business Korea*, May 2, 2016; and "Hozour nakhostvazir asbagh koreye jenoobi dar Hamshahri," [Former South Korean Premier Visits Hamshahri] *Hamshahri*, February 29, 2016, p. 1.
92 "A New Path for Korea and the Middle East," *Business Korea*, December 15, 2009; "Abe Tries to Fill Korea's Vacuum in Middle East," *Korea Times*, February 10, 2015;

As compared to her Mideast-savvy predecessor, Lee Myung-bak, Park had scored very little in the Middle East and was at risk of leaving office without much to boast about in the region. Of course, the wider Middle East region had long been a low priority for Korean leaders, though Lee had rectified that shortcoming by paying frequent high-profile visits and signing dozens of lucrative contracts for Koreans in both the public and private sectors.[93] But in spite of impediments such as Park's gender and lack of experience in the region, she had set out to continue the ROK's recent drive for a "second boom" in the Middle East, and the official visit to the Persian Gulf country was expected to contribute to that cherished agenda.[94]

There were, additionally, other sanguine interpretations with regard to broader impacts of Park's travel to Tehran. Some observers contended, no matter how naively, that Park's warmer approach to a major Middle Eastern power could ultimately raise South Korea's foreign policy profile in a wider world.[95] Another group accentuated how the trip might impact relations with North Korea. They particularly underscored the recently-signed Iranian nuclear deal and how Park's visit to Tehran could put additional pressure on Pyongyang in favor of a general denuclearization of the Korean Peninsula, favored by Seoul. Moreover, South Korea could further isolate the communist regime of Pyongyang, such observers argued, by fostering better political ties with a major friend of North Korea.[96] No matter how valid all these ex-

---

and "Daechungdong wegyo sae jipyeong yeon Iran pangmun," [Iran Visit Opens New Horizon toward the Middle East] *Seoul Kyeongje*, May 4, 2016.

93 Shirzad Azad, "Déjà vu Diplomacy: South Korea's Middle East Policy under Lee Myung-bak," *Contemporary Arab Affairs*, Vol. 6, No. 4 (November 2013), pp. 552–566.

94 "Invest in Iran," *Korea Times*, January 25, 2016; "Hyundai, Kia Seek to Regain Iranian Market," *KBS World Radio*, January 27, 2016; "Korea to Boost Economic Cooperation with Iran," *Business Korea*, January 22, 2016; "Biz Leaders Ask Park to Expand Summit Diplomacy on Economy," *Yonhap News Agency*, May 11, 2016; "'Hangugkieobdeul Iraneseo '2cha chungdongbum' kyeongheomhal su isseul geos'," ['Korean Companies will be Able to Experience 'the 2nd Middle East Boom' in Iran'] *Hankyoreh*, April 21, 2016; and "Feat from Trip to Iran: Following President Park to Iran Works out for IRISYS," *Business Korea*, June 30, 2016.

95 "Excelsior with Iran!" *Korea Times*, May 10, 2016.

96 "Park May Gain Iranian Support over Nuke Issue," *Korea Times*, April 29, 2016; "Park Calls for Iran's Cooperation over N. Korea's Nuclear Ambitions," *Yonhap News Agency*, May 2, 2016; "Iran President Opposes North Korea's Nuke Program," *Korea Times*, May 2, 2016; and "Seoul Picking off Pyongyang's Friends," *Nikkei Asian Review*, June 14, 2016.

---

pectations might have been, though, the ROK had to first meet various challenges in both initiating and cultivating closer political relations with Iran.[97]

Contingent Upon: Political Perturbation And Bewildering Bafflegab

In the long run, South Korea's wish to rekindle its multifaceted political ties with Iran will certainly depend on a whole host of nettlesome issues. First and foremost, the ROK would ineluctably be dependent on the whims of the Americans for any significant improvement in its political interactions with Iran. No matter how adamantly South Koreans strive to assert themselves as independent players in both regional and international politics, the United States will continue to hold considerable sway over major aspects of the ROK's security and foreign policies for the foreseeable future. Moreover, as long as Koreans are unable to manage without the endless assistance of America in East Asia in general and the Korean Peninsula in particular, they will have little hope but to go on relying on the United States in other equally, if not far more, complex and dangerous regions. In the unfathomable world of Middle Eastern politics, the Koreans will particularly have to lean on their American ally for strategic, political, and economic reasons.[98] The stakes are obviously higher when the ROK needs to carefully and productively deal with a major and perplexing power in the Middle East such as Iran.

On the Iranian side, things are not very predictable either. Friendly and close political relations with US-orientated states such as the ROK will have to wait for a major rapprochement between Iran and the West in general and the United States in particular. Besides that, the signed agreements and promises made between Iran and South Korea are hardly water-tight; their fulfilment will largely depend on the political will of the Iranians. South Koreans indubitably want better political interactions with Iran, primarily for

97 "South Korean President Seeks Iran's Help on Pyongyang Sanctions," *Wall Street Journal*, May 2, 2016; "Iran Leader Urges Move to Nuclear Weapons-free Korean Peninsula," *Asahi Shimbun*, May 3, 2016; "Park-Khamenei Meeting Adds Pressure on North Korea," *Korea Times*, May 3, 2016; and "South Korea Courts Isolated North's Old Friends in Push for Change," *Reuters*, June 7, 2016.

98 "S. Korea Becoming Heavily Dependent on Oil from Persian Gulf: U.S. Report," *Yonhap News Agency*, June 10, 2007; "Our Unconventional-oil Future," *Korea Joongang Daily*, July 2, 2013; "Korea, Middle East Eye Stronger Partnership," *Korea Herald*, April 24, 2015; "Mideast Crisis: Korea Has Become More Dependent on Crude Oil from the Middle East," *Business Korea*, May 19, 2015; and "Korea Imports More Iranian Oil," *Chosun Ilbo*, November 7, 2016.

the sake of improving their economic interests in Iran. But there is absolutely no guarantee that Tehran will be prepared to meet all of its economic commitments with regard to the flurry of documents the country signed during Park's visit in early May 2016.[99] In fact, things may even move in the reverse direction, since the present situation has the potential to make things harder for South Korea, in case it fails to satisfy Tehran's financial and technical expectations in exchange for access to the lucrative Iranian markets.

One other serious matter facing South Korea is how to make up for the many lost opportunities, particularly in information and cultural areas. Over the past decades, the ROK media and press have recycled a load of negative and anti-Iranian tropes for strategic and political purposes dear to the country's ruling elites. One has to personally and meticulously delve into the archives of certain Korean newspapers and magazines of popular subjects to find out about this bitter reality concerning Iran and Iranians.[100] Although things have slightly changed for the better in recent years, the standoffish attitude of average South Korean citizens toward Iranians, and generally the peoples of the Middle East, continue to impede relations.[101] As a case in point, on the eve of Park's visit to Iran, the *Korean Times* published another Iran-bashing piece tinged with the caricature of a rather repulsive-looking Arab to, as usual, instill the belief in its readers that Iranians and Arabs are to be tarred with the same brush, although they are entirely different peoples.[102]

As a corollary to that, friendly feelings and good ties between the two countries have so far been largely constrained to the realm of diplomacy and

99 "South Korea, Iran to Sign 44 MoUs," *Trend News Agency,* May 2, 2016; "Questions Arise over Massive Iran Contracts," *Korea Times,* May 3, 2016; and "Park Basks in Afterglow of Success in Iran," *Korea Joongang Daily,* May 5, 2016.
100 "Reasons Not to Trust Iran on Nukes," *Korea Joongang Daily,* September 27, 2013; "Poignant Resistance," *Korea Times,* April 4, 2014; "Iranian Hackers 'Targeted Korean Air'," *Chosun Ilbo,* December 4, 2014; "The Iran Deal: Four Big Questions," *Korea Joongang Daily,* July 20, 2015; "Iran Already Cheating," *Korea Times,* December 14, 2015; and "Tohin bazikon koreye jenoobi be mardom Iran," [South Korean Player Insulted Iranian People] *Tabnak,* October 8, 2016.
101 "North Korea Presumed to be Negotiating Arms Deal with Middle East Terrorist Groups," *Arirang News,* August 6, 2014; and "Iranian FM Says Nukes Can't Guarantee Regime Security," *Chosun Ilbo,* November 9, 2015.
102 "When in Iran, Do as the Iranians Do," *Korea Times,* April 18, 2016. Sometime in fall 2014, this author encountered, over lunch time, a Seoul National University's professor of International Relations who surprised to hear for the first time that Iranians are not Arab and their spoken national language is Persian and not Arabic. Such poor understanding of Iran and Iranians by an educated Korean holding a PhD from a top American university could indeed talk volumes about what average Korean citizens knew about the Persian Gulf country, and generally the Middle East region.

relevant economic centers of power. Almost all officials and influential people active in these areas did their utmost to always present a rather positive picture about how the two countries behaved toward each other without caring much about what their affiliated society in large thought. As a matter of fact, there happened to be very little, if any, ordinary people to people interactions between the two sides since a great deal of bilateral connections were either governmental or state-sponsored relations in one way or another.[103] Rectifying such a wearisome impediment requires careful thought and planning, and achieving desired outcomes is neither cheap nor guaranteed. A vexing dilemma is that South Koreans may take steps in such a hopeful direction only to again preserve or enhance their vested economic interests in Iran, similar to what they have so far done with regard to their relentless mission of cultural promotion in Iran.

Last but not least is the issue of the ROK's political relationship with Tehran. This relationship is conditioned not only by the United States and Iran. The East Asian country's expanding interests in a wider Middle East may compel it to eventually adopt more transparent policies and straightforward behaviors with regard to forging new alliances in the region. Until now, the ROK has often strived to hide behind political courtesy and diplomatic mumbo jumbo in order to safeguard its interests among rival political groups, particularly in the Persian Gulf region.

South Korea was lucky enough to survive relatively easily as long as the strategic and political competition were not corrosive to its essential interests there. Partly this was thanks to the endless political support as well as the security umbrella of the United States. Since the Koreans can hardly count on this rather protected environment in the greater Middle East region to last forever, only time will reveal whether or not they can adjust to changing circumstances in the future.

---

103 While the Korean government is willing to facilitate as much as possible and chip away at the bureaucratic and visa red tape for Iranian merchants and distributors who contribute to the Korean economy handsomely, it has yet to come up with bold initiatives in order to smooth the way for genuine people to people interactions among other social groups. "Sodoor ravadid tejari korye jenoobi baray tojjar irani tay moddat 24 ta 48 saat," [Issuance of South Korean Trade Visa for Iranian Merchants within 24 to 48hrs] *Audit & Inspection Society of Iran*, August 28, 2017.

The Balancing Act: Attachment To Both Iranians And Arabs

In the midst of Park's Iran visit, a number of influential Korean newspapers and media outlets warned her government about risking the ROK's overall interests in the Middle East by appearing overly friendly toward Iranians. Pundit particularly voiced their concerns about potential backlash on the ROK's bilateral relationship with the Arab countries, especially Saudi Arabia.[104] This was a major reason why Park swiftly dispatched her prime minister to the kingdom of Saudi Arabia, less than three weeks after returning from Tehran.[105] South Koreans simply wanted to convince the Arabs that any improved ties with Iran were not going to come at their expense, particularly at a time when Tehran and Riyadh were very tense with each other. The relationship had been strained since Saudi Arabia's diplomatic mission in Iran had been ransacked by a number of conservative forces unhappy with the Arab country's divisive policies in the Middle East.[106]

Basically, South Korea's Iran policy has long been subject to implicit and explicit pressures from various pro-American, pro-Israeli, and pro-Arab lobbies both inside and outside the ROK.[107] Although Korean companies with large interests in Iran have by and large been the strongest, and essentially the only, pro-Iran lobby in South Korea, they too have sometimes failed to withstand the relentless systematic pressure and intimidation from the foregoing circles of power and influence.[108] Even some so-called research and

104 For instance, see: "Saudi–Iranian Rivalry May Hamper Seoul," *Korea Times*, April 5, 2015; "'Iranian Rush' Poses Diplomatic Challenges," *Korea Herald*, May 1, 2016; "Middle East Diplomacy Put to Test," *Korea Times*, May 2, 2016; and "Headlong into Iran," *Korea Joongang Daily*, May 9, 2016.
105 "Fast-growing Gulf Carriers Making Inroads into Korea," *Korea Herald*, April 18, 2014; "Korea Walks Tightrope between Iran, Saudi Arabia," *Korea Times*, May 9, 2016; and "PM Set to Meet with Saudi Arabia's King for Talks on Cooperation," *Yonhap News Agency*, May 22, 2016.
106 "The Koreans, the Arabs and Striking Similarities," *Al Arabiya*, November 25, 2010; "Keen to Boost UAE–South Korea Strategic Ties: Khalifa," *Emirates 24/7*, March 13, 2011; "Lessons from South Korea," *Al Arabiya*, October 31, 2013; "GCC–South Korean Ties Reviewed," *Bahrain News Agency*, May 27, 2014; "GCC, ROK Sign Strategic Cooperation Deal," *Kuwait News Agency*, September 27, 2014; and "Korea Pursues Closer Ties with Saudi Arabia," *Korea Times*, May 19, 2016.
107 "Arab Views on Iran Surprise Some Experts," *The National*, December 12, 2014; "What the Persian Gulf States Want: Iran Kept at Bay," *Los Angeles Times*, May 9, 2015; and "Gulf Arabs Fear Iran with Cash as Much as Iran with the Bomb," *Financial Times*, May 12, 2015.
108 "GCC Builds up Its Asia Strategy," *Gulf News*, October 4, 2014; "Gulf Nations Focus on More Investments in East Asia," *Gulf Times*, November 6, 2014; "GCC FMs Meet Korean Counterpart on Security, Economic Ties," *Kuwait News Agency*, October

academic bodies such as the Asan Institute for Policy Studies (*Asan cheong-chaeg yeonguwon*) have openly demonstrated their rather anti-Iran opinions and sentiments in different ways favorable to the taste of people active for the pro-American camp inside or outside the ROK. Of course, the approach and dynamism of those lobbies have significantly transformed over time as South Korea's overall interests in and foreign policy orientation toward the greater Middle East region have undergone new developments as well.[109]

Roughly from the 1960s until the early 1990s, when Seoul normalized its diplomatic ties with Tel Aviv, the ROK's greatest difficulty in the wider Middle East region was how to balance its interests in Israel against those in the opposite group of Mideast countries. The East Asian country sometimes had to walk a tightrope in order to avoid seriously angering either party at the cost of its own vital economic interests. Even when the collapse of the Pahlavi dynasty in Iran and the ensuing ascendancy of the Islamic Repub-lic stoked up some fierce anti-Israeli policies in Tehran, nevertheless South Korea's main focus in the region was on safeguarding its interests both in Israel and in countries hostile to Israel.[110] There were also some concerns in Seoul with regard to pushing back against North Korea's growing presence in the Middle East, but this issue was not really pivotal. The North Korean factor gradually became less pressing, and the considerations governing the dual-track diplomatic line also shifted.[111]

After the ROK established its political relationship with Israel, and many Arab countries were also forced to reconsider their policies toward the Jewish state, the Iranian–Arab dichotomy gradually became a new political and ideological reality, replacing the erstwhile Arab–Israeli chasm in the re-

1, 2015; and "Saudi Arabia Cuts Ties with Iran After Embassy Attack," *Khaleej Times*, January 4, 2016.

109 "'Win-win' Situation as Middle East–South Korea Ties Enter New Era," *The National*, October 23, 2013; "Abu Dhabi Gets Taste of Korean Cuisine," *Gulf News*, February 7, 2014; "Arab Medical Tourists Spend Big in Korea," *Chosun Ilbo*, November 4, 2014; "GCC Secretary General Meets Korean Ambassador," *Bahrain News Agency*, November 9, 2014; and "New Gov't Center to Support Business with Iran," *Chosun Ilbo*, January 26, 2016.

110 "Dubai and South Korea Sign Joint Investments Deal," *Financial Times*, August 18, 2014; and "New Era in Already Warm Korea–Iran Relations," *Korea Joongang Daily*, April 28, 2016.

111 "Iran, Israel, and the North Korea Analogy," *The National Interest*, May 19, 2015; "Jejudo Woos Saudi Billionaire in Bid to Host Four Seasons," *Korea Herald*, May 17, 2016; and "Dubai to Host Korea Expo 2016," *Khaleej Times*, October 18, 2016.

gion.[112] The Iranian–Arab schism had its own roots harkening back hundreds of years, but its corrosive reverberations had been contained by various politico-economic and cultural centers of power in contemporary history.[113] South Korea, like most other states, inevitably had to strive to maintain some sort of neutrality to both parties. Even when the Asian country's vital interests dictated otherwise or when its real position was already crystal clear to everyone, the ROK had little option but to officially stick to its neutral position *vis-à-vis* Iran and the Arab countries. Even in routine communication this delicate problem has to be negotiated, as when South Korea needs to refer to Arab countries that are located in what is generally called the Persian Gulf region.

Like Japan, South Korea has been adamant in using the term "Middle East" when referring to any country in the region. This policy has been particularly consistent since the Iraqi invasion of Kuwait in 1990. In reporting on the military conflict that followed, the South Korean foreign ministry instructed the media simply to say only "the Gulf" when referring to the region.[114] Although the waterway of the Persian Gulf is as large as the geographical size of the entire Korean Peninsula, South Koreans steadfastly pretend that they do not see it whenever they cover a political development or news story related to the region. Instead, they usually refer to the "Middle East" even when their leaders tour only one country, as was the case during Park's visit to Iran in May 2016. The ROK's closest allies in the West, the United States in particular, make no such effort to appear even handed.[115]

New Dynamism In The Tehran–Pyongyang Partnership

As for North Korea, Ahmadinejad and his key ministers never visited the country, and they hardly ever discussed in public any important issue related

---

112 "Analysis: Pyongyang Nuke Test May Also be Iranian," *Jerusalem Post*, February 13, 2013; "Netanyahu: A nuclear-armed Iran Means 'Another 50 North Koreas," *Korea Times*, October 2, 2013; "Israel Warns of N.Korea–Iran Nuclear Link," *Chosun Ilbo*, November 26, 2014; and "Reviving the Iran–North Korea Axis," *LobeLog*, August 6, 2015.

113 "The Demise of the Iranian Bogeyman Makes Israeli's Position More Difficult," *Independent*, September 27, 2013; and "The Cold Arab–Israeli Alliance against Iran," *World Affairs Journal*, April 19, 2016.

114 "'Persian Gulf' out, 'Gulf' in," *Korea Herald*, January 22, 1991, p. 2.

115 Lawrence G. Potter, *The Persian Gulf in History* (New York: Palgrave Macmillan, 2009).

to Iran's relations with the DPRK.[116] Whenever they were interviewed with regard to controversies in Tehran's ties with Pyongyang, they vehemently denied any wrongdoing and instead boasted about their own country's indigenous capabilities to meet any technological needs, including missile technology or nuclear energy equipment.

Under the Rouhani government, Iran has been even less inclined to highlight its interactions with the communist regime of North Korea.[117] As compared to a number of high-profile diplomatic and non-political delegations from the DPRK to Tehran, few, if any, important officials from Iran have visited North Korea in recent years.[118] At some point during the nuclear negotiations, moreover, the Iranian foreign ministry was even willing to scuttle a planned visit to Tehran by a top North Korean delegation, mainly in order to make more progress in Tehran's crucial talks with the 5+1 party.[119]

One other significant point was Iran's explicit support for the denuclearization of the Korean Peninsula during Park's official negotiations with Rouhani in Tehran. Nevertheless, the news was broadcast with great fanfare by the South Korean media and this was interpreted by some as a sign of Iran's further "distancing" itself from North Korea in the wake of successfully signing the nuclear deal, even though the DPRK preferred, in fact, to ignore

---

116 "In Tehran, All Eyes on North Korea," *Foreign Policy in Focus*, May 14, 2013; and "North Korea and Iran: A Spiritual Alliance," *Asia Times*, November 21, 2013.

117 Probably a major exception was an occasion when Kim Yong-nam, the President of the Presidium of the Supreme People's Assembly of North Korea, visited Tehran to attend Rouhani's second inauguration ceremony held on August 5, 2017. Dubbed by the Iranian media the "mysterious guest" of the inauguration ceremony, the top North Korean official made a rather long sojourn in Iran, raising speculations about the possibility of critical areas of cooperation and joint activities between the two countries. See: "North Korea's No. 2' Official Strengthens Ties with Iran as UN Hits Pyongyang with New Sanctions," *CNBC*, August 4, 2017; "'Mehman marmooz' marasem tahlif ke bood," [Who was the 'Mysterious Guest' of Inauguration Ceremony] *Iranian Students' News Agency (ISNA)*, August 6, 2017; and "Rouhani dar didar raeis presidium majmaeh ali khalgh korye shomali che goft?" [What Did Rouhani Say in Meeting with the President of the Presidium of the Supreme People's Assembly of North Korea?] *Aftab News*, August 7, 2017.

118 "FMs of Iran, DPRK Meet in Tehran," *Tasnim News Agency*, February 24, 2014; "Iran Looks to Boost Asia Ties as N.Korea FM Visits," *Bangkok Post*, September 17, 2014; "Iran Voices Opposition to N. Korea's Nuclear Program," *Yonhap News Agency*, May 3, 2016; and "Iran Complies with Resolution on N Korea, Prepares Implementation Report," *Mehr News Agency*, July 2, 2016.

119 "Ettehad cyberi Irav va koreye shomali," [Cyber Alliance of Iran and North Korea] *Tabnak*, September 4, 2012; "Maneh safar heiat kore shomali be Iran taid shod," [Prohibition of North Korean Delegation's Visit to Iran Confirmed] *Jahan News*, February 17, 2014; and "Didar vazir kharejeh koreye shomali ba Rouhani," [North Korean Foreign Minister Meets Rouhani] *Tabnak*, September 16, 2014.

Rouhani's statement. But it was something of an exaggeration to claim that Iran was going to significantly dissociate from North Korea any time soon.[120] The Rouhani government may have some other priorities and preferences in foreign policy, but it is not in a position to disrupt Iran's connections to foreign partners like the DPRK. And in any event, such a major shift would not take place as a result of Tehran's closer political ties with Seoul or because of South Korea's diplomatic campaign to drive a wedge between Iran and North Korea.[121]

Meanwhile, the Iranian nuclear deal with the 5+1 party has been widely lauded as a model for resolving the North Korean nuclear problem.[122] Influential people in the West and the East, from top political leaders to academics and policy wonks, have asked the DPRK on multiple occasions to emulate the Iranians in order to find a peaceful solution for its nuclear controversy.[123] Interesting enough, the top leadership in North Korea has yet to express its candid view on the Iranian nuclear deal. But it is understandable that they are not that happy about it, since the deal which Iran agreed to has put additional pressure on Pyongyang. Quite to the contrary, the DPRK has recently resorted to occasional "nuclear tests" to make up for its further political isolation. North Korea feels that it is in the crosshairs for insisting it has an inalienable right to develop nuclear weapons, while it feels that its sovereignty and territorial integrity are besieged and threatened. [124]

120 "Nuclear North Korea: 6 Ways It Differs from Iran," *Christian Science Monitor*, December 5, 2013; "Can Iranian Nuke Talks Affect N.K. Issue?" *Korea Herald*, November 26, 2014; "Iran Deal's Impact on N. Korea," *Korea Times*, July 19, 2015; and "North Korea's Military Partnerships under Threat?" *38 North*, June 17, 2016.
121 "Iran Lessons Key for North Korea," *CNN*, January 8, 2016; and "Iranian Lesson for NK," *Korea Times*, May 4, 2016.
122 "After Iran Agreement, Seoul Must Lead on N. Korea Nuke Dialogue Efforts," *The Hankyoreh*, April 4, 2015; "Iran Nuclear Deal: The Real Lessons from North Korea," *Christian Science Monitor*, May 13, 2015; "Saenuri Urges N. Korea to Join Iran's Path," *Yonhap News Agency*, April 4, 2015; "Gov't Urges NK to Follow Path of Iran for Denuclearization," *Korea Times*, July 14, 2015; and "North Korea Can Learn from Iran Nuclear Deal, U.S. Says," *Reuters*, April 19, 2016;
123 "Iran Nuclear Deal Leaves N. Korea Exposed," *Chosun Ilbo*, July 15, 2015; "British Foreign Minister Hopes Iran Deal will Help Resolve N.K. Nuclear Issue," *Yonhap News Agency*, August 10, 2015; "FM Hopes N. Korea will Learn Lesson from Iranian Deal," *KBS World Radio*, November 8, 2015; "Minister Urges NK to Learn from Iran," *Korea Times*, November 8, 2015; and "Time for Iran-style Talks with N. Korea: FM Yun," *Yonhap News Agency*, January 26, 2016.
124 "North Korea Takes a Tip from Iran's 'Charm Offensive'?" *Forbes*, October 24, 2014; "5 Reasons Why the Iran Framework Isn't a Template for North Korea," *Wall Street Journal*, April 3, 2015; "The Worst Agreement in U.S. Diplomatic History," *Washington Post*, July 2, 2015; "With US-Iran Deal, It's Only North Korea that is Left,"

Whether or not North Korea will be willing or will be forced to follow Iran's example on the nuclear question, the communist DPRK has been quietly undergoing considerable change in recent years. Of course, such developments are seen more in the areas of soft economic and cultural issues rather than sensitive strategic and political matters.[125]

As soon as Kim Jong-un replaced his ailing father, Kim Jong-il, who died in December 2011, the political establishment in Pyongyang embarked upon a gradual transition toward more non-state economic forces as well as materially-charged cultural trends. Even the North Korean Workers' Party (KWP) unexpectedly held a congress in May 2016 (its first since 1980). Although much was said about that crucial gathering's political agenda and its final declaration, first and foremost the congregation of the DPRK's top elites endorsed a series of obvious changes and paved the way for additional reforms in some other areas which seem to be too sensitive to be discussed in public for now.[126] The reforms put in place were quite varied in scope and size, ranging from embracing a more capitalistic economy at the national level to erecting more skyscrapers and shopping malls in big cities such as Pyongyang. Managers and farmers in the so-called private sector were encouraged to "do business creatively," and there was a cautious promotion of what some pundits dub "crony capitalism" in the public sector. Some other measures included axing government subsidies, more monetization of the economy, relaxing price controls in favor of the principle of "supply and demand," and allowing more foreign tourists and foreign investments, etc. In sum, the air of renewal and reform is real in the DPRK, and it's seen from the hairstyle of its leader down to the growing popularity of plastic surgery and luxury goods among its well-to-do women.

On top of that, Koreans on both sides of the DMZ have been artificially separated from each other for some seven decades, but their mental and social sinews have not fundamentally differed in many ways. True that the society in the ROK has changed dramatically in more than half a century;

The Hankyoreh, July 15, 2015; "Iran-style Nuclear Deal for North Korea? Kim Signals No.," Christian Science Monitor, July 21, 2015; and "N. Korea Should Heed Iranian Leader's Advice," Chosun Ilbo, May 3, 2016.

125 Norman D. Levin, The Shape of Korea's Future: South Korean Attitudes Toward Unification and Long-Term Security Issues (Santa Monica, CA: RAND, 1999), p. 13.

126 Ken E. Gause, North Korea under Kim Chong-il: Power, Politics, and Prospects for Change (Santa Barbara, CA: Praeger, 2011), pp. 119–121.

nevertheless, the people of North Korea have been only artificially and arbitrarily kept from following their literal brethren in the south in accumulating
money, chasing materialism, showing off wealth, seeking pleasure, etc.[127] As
a matter of fact, people in the DPRK are more prone to such proclivities and
they only need time and opportunity to prove their thirst and hunger for a
completely different lifestyle than the one has long been imposed upon them
by the Korean Workers' Party in Pyongyang. Even many ordinary North Korean citizens have already drifted toward wealth accumulation and sybaritic
lifestyles, which the well-placed elites of their society have long pursued in
one way to another.[128]

As Iran takes a new approach in its foreign policy and as North Korea
adopts changes in its domestic policies, such developments should have
some effect on the way the two parties manage their bilateral ties.[129] Iran may
no longer need Pyongyang's close cooperation in military and nuclear energy
technologies, while the DPRK may feel abashed to put much faith in Iran's
political support for its nuclear ambitions.[130] But as the Chinese example has
long proved, Iran can still remain an important political ally for North Korea
on a wide range of other issues.[131] The Persian Gulf country will be equally

127 "The Secret Capitalist Economy of North Korea," *CNN*, July 19, 2009; "Think
Tanks See Hope in N. Korean Capitalism," *Chosun Ilbo*, January 3, 2014; and "Kim
Jong-un Urged to Cater to New Rich," *Korea Times*, November 17, 2015.
128 "Foreign Porn Flows Into N. Korea," *Chosun Ilbo*, October 18, 2010; "Chinese
Media: 'Pyongyang is Exclusively for the Privileged'," *Dong-A Ilbo*, December 9, 2014;
"Pyongyang Bling: The Rise of North Korea's Consumer Comrades," *Reuters*, June 3,
2015; and "In North Korea, 'Things Have Changed A Lot'," *The Hankyoreh*, November
19, 2015.
129 "Officials of Blacklisted N. Korea Firm Visit Iran after UN Slaps Sanctions:
Source," *Yonhap News Agency*, March 28, 2016; and "Iran va koreye shomali dar jeb-
hei vahed aleih America," [Iran and North Korea in United Front against America]
Tabnak, January 30, 2017.
130 In an interview with an Iranian news agency in May 2017, Mohsen Rafighdoost,
Minister of the Revolutionary Guards from 1982 to 1989 and a key player behind the
Persian Gulf country's military purchases during the Iran–Iraq War, stated that "We
have always had good and agreeable relations with North Korea, and despite the geographical distance between Iran and this Asian country our cordial relationship will
continue in the future as well...we are going to throw our political support behind
North Korea for the time to come...right now, we do not need arms connections to the
North Koreans, we maintained such interactions in the war period and they helped
us a lot, but we no longer require any country's assistance for our defense." "Aya Iran
hamchenan az korye shomali selah mikharad?" [Does Iran Still Buy Weapons from
North Korea?] *Mizan Online News Agency*, May 27, 2017.
131 "North Korea, Iran Agree to Deepen Strategic Ties: Insider," *Global Security
Newswire*, July 25, 2012; "North Korea's Middle East Pivot," *The Diplomat*, July 29, 2014;
"Iran et al. Censure UN Resolution on North Korea," *Press TV*, November 19, 2014;

crucial to help Pyongyang with regard to its recent drive for gradual economic and financial transformation in order to ultimately reunify with South Korea.[132] Even if such a reunification were to take place abruptly and arbitrarily sometime soon, Iran would still be in a position to furnish resources to facilitate the growth and development programs that would follow, no matter which political party would be in charge under a unified Korea.[133]

Regardless of the dynamism adumbrated earlier and in spite of any sanguine perspective about a foreseeable future, Iran's atypical relations with North Korea, and even Tehran's unorthodox connections to South Korea, can neither be taken for granted nor are such unusual ties impervious to torrents of unanticipated events, incidents, rumors, allegations, inspections, or inquiries. Because of the nature of modern Iranian politics and the way the Persian Gulf country has managed its foreign policies vis-à-vis the Eastern and Western countries over the past four decades, a large dossier can always be produced to demonstrate one point or another about Iranian–Korean interactions, though a similar task can be taken on with regard to Iran's other foreign partners or its adversaries. This is exactly what happened in early 2018 when a maritime commercial vessel owned by Iran mysteriously encountered a tragic incident and perished.

The Sepulchral Sinking Of the Sanchi: The Plot Thickens
In Iran's Peculiar Ties To Two Koreas

On January 6, 2018, the news splashed across headlines around the world that the Sanchi, an Iranian-owned oil tanker, had collided with CF Crystal, a Hong Kong-flagged cargo ship, some 300 km east of Shanghai in the East China Sea. The ill-fated tanker caught fire upon collision and eventually sank on January 14 after burning haplessly for more than a week. The Sanchi's pitiable 32 crew members, including 30 Iranians and two Bangladeshi sea-

"North Korea's Takeaway from the Iran Nuclear Talks," *Forbes*, May 21, 2015; and "North Korea's Real Lessons for Iran," *New York Times*, April 10, 2015.

132 "Iranian Leader Willing to Mediate between Koreas," *Yonhap News Agency*, January 27, 2014; "Dialogue Essential to Settle Dispute between North and South Korea: Iran," *Tehran Times*, January 13, 2015; and "FM Yun to Visit Iran, Discuss N.K. Nukes," *Yonhap News Agency*, November 3, 2015.

133 "Safar heiat parlemani Iran be koreye shomali," [Iran Parliamentary Delegate Visits North Korea] *Tabnak*, July 28, 2013; "Iran Backs Unity between North, South Korea: Zarif," *Press TV*, February 25, 2014; and "Could North Korea Benefit from Middle East Shifts?" *The Diplomat*, August 24, 2015.

farers, all died straight away; the rescue team managed to recover only three bodies of the victims before the wreckage sank to a depth of 115 meters.[134] There was certainly no hope of finding survivors any longer, while the financial costs of the oil tanker was estimated to be around $110 million, including $50 million for the vessel itself and $60 million for its full cargo of 960,000 barrels of natural-gas condensate.[135]

There were, however, many mysteries and unanswered questions about the Sanchi, and the deep sea was a secure place to bury them all at once. In fact, the decade-long lifespan of the oil tanker had been as mysterious as its perplexing final days of forlorn burning over the bloody waters of the East China Sea. At the time of collision, the Sanchi bore the Panamanian flag despite being operated by the National Iranian Tanker Company (NITC) since 2008. Before being renamed the Sanchi in August 2013, it had changed names several times, including Saman, Sepid, Gardenia, and Seahorse. The tanker had been reflagged from Malta to Tuvalu in 2012, before being reflagged again to Tanzania in April 2014 and finally to Panama in July 2016. Whether such frequent changes of name and registration had anything to do with circumventing sanctions or more conventional cost-saving tricks in maritime transportation, it adds up to a colorful story.[136]

Meanwhile, the sinking immediately opened a Pandora's Box. It is still hard to repudiate the rumors in full or to substantiate them indisputably. Once the Sanchi caught fire, some people, among them a number of Iranian parliamentarians, claimed that the vessel had been attacked by missiles fired by the United States.[137] This introduced confusing and worrisome questions, including the possibility that the Sanchi might not actually have been carrying a cargo of natural-gas condensate for Hanwha Total, the South Korean petrochemicals company, as had been reported. Instead, they claimed that

134 "Taeid margh hameh sarneshinan Sanchi," [Death of All Crew Members on Sanchi Confirmed] *Shargh Daily*, January 15, 2018, p. 1.
135 "Akharin saat margbar Sanchi," [Final Deadly Hours of Sanchi] *Shargh Daily*, March 4, 2018, pp. 1, 4.
136 "Iranian Oil Tanker Sinks after Burning for more than One Week," *Telegraph*, January 14, 2018; and "Iranian Oil Tanker Sinks a Week after Fiery Crash," *New York Times*, January 15, 2018, p. A6.
137 "Barrasi yek shayeeh dagh ke az majles shoroo shodeh; aya Sanchi mored hamleh amrikaeiha gharar gerefteh ast?" [Reviewing a Hot Rumor which Started from the Parliament; Has Sanchi Come under Attack by Americans?] *Tabnak*, January 14, 2018.

the real destination was North Korea, and that the Americans wanted to stop the vessel before it could reach the territorial waters of the DPRK.[138]

The relationship between Washington and Pyongyang was already tense, and the Trump administration had just levied a new round of sanctions against the communist state, nominally because of its repeated missile and nuclear tests. Among other steps, curtailing the energy supply to North Korea was supposed to be part of the punitive measures initiated by Washington and its close allies in the region. And after all, the United States had previously shot down Iran Air 655, a civilian flight, on July 3, 1988, killing all 290 people on board.[139] Such somber recollections made the narrative of a US strike on the Sanchi easily convincing to many people.[140]

Another relevant rumor, however, absolved the United States from any wrongdoing against the Sanchi, but North Korea was still at the kernel of its narrative. According to this thought-provoking view, the Iranian government was secretly and silently assisting its North Korean friend, which was already in dire need of oil because of the UN-imposed sanctions. The people who raised this speculation alleged that the Sanchi had collided with the Hong Kong-flagged cargo ship simply because Tehran had ordered its oil tanker to shut down its maritime signals and warning devices in order not to be recognized and located by the radars before arriving in the safe waters of the DPRK.[141] In this case, the culpability of the Iranian government would be clear.[142]

China, however, became another major target of rumors and widespread wrath among Iranians. They particularly accused China of shirking its obvious responsibility to quickly put an end to the inferno which had engulfed

---

138 "Mooj shayeeh pas az fajeeh," [Wave of Rumor after Disaster] *Khorasan Daily*, January 16, 2018, pp. 1, 13; and "Taallol chin shayeeh ast," [Chinese Procrastination is Gossip] *Shargh Daily*, January 22, 2018, pp. 1, 4.

139 "The Forgotten Story of Iran Air Flight 655," *Washington Post*, October 16, 2013.

140 "Shellik mooshak be Sanchi dastansoraei ast," [Missile Attack against Sanchi is Fairy Tale] *Tabnak*, January 16, 2018; and "Iran 'shayeeh hamleh' be naftkesh Sanchi ra rad kar," [Iran Denied 'Attack Rumor' against Sanchi Oil Tanker] *Deutsche Welle*, January 16, 2018.

141 "Vakonesh vezarat kharejeh be shayeat darbareh safar naftkesh irani be maghsad korye shomali: Maghsad naftkesh Sanchi korye jenoobi bood," [Foreign Ministry's Reaction to Rumors about North Korea as the Destination of Iranian Oil Tanker: South Korea was the Destination of Sanchi Oil Tanker] *Ebtekar*, January 16, 2018, p. 1.

142 "Maghsad naftkesh Sanchi koja bood?" [Where was Sanchi's Destination?] *Tabnak*, January 15, 2018.

the Sanchi and its unfortunate crew members.[143] As the rescue operation dragged on to no avail for several days, the citizenry grew restless, condemning the Chinese for sacrificing the oil tanker as well as its cargo and crews due to their own selfish environmental concerns in the East China Sea.[144] China, as some claimed, had done next to nothing by letting the entire cargo go up in smoke before the oil tanker sank in deep waters. In the view of some other observers, the communist Chinese government was either concealing its own direct role in the incident or it was just helping the Iranian government, and possibly even the North Korean communist regime, to hush up the whole scandalous affair and its damaging details.[145]

The last but not least scapegoat was the Iranian government itself. A short while before the Sanchi caught fire, the Iranian government had managed to weather a new storm of public protests which had taken place in various cities throughout the country beginning on December 28, 2017, and continuing well into 2018.[146] It was, therefore, very convenient for some people, many of them among the opposition groups outside the country, to take advantage of the Sanchi incident as proof of the Iranian government's failures. They argued that the government, alone or in close cooperation with China, had orchestrated the whole tragic event as a false flag of sorts in order to skillfully deflect attention from the recent public demonstrations. As the Sanchi sank, taking with it any relevant evidence, in the perception of its adherents this line of argumentation could cover the possibility of a range of convoluted conspiracies involving one or more governments.[147]

---

143 "Ravayat chini az fajeeh Sanchi," [Chinese Narrative of Sanchi Disaster] *Khorasan Daily*, January 21, 2018, pp. 1, 13; and "Ba hozoor namayandegan Iran, chin, Panama, va Hong Kong; Jabeh syah Sanchi baz shod," [In the Presence of Iran, China, Panama, and Hong Kong Representatives; Black Box of Sanchi was Opened] *Mardomsalari*, January 25, 2018, p. 1.
144 "Fajeeh Sanchi az aghaz hadeseh ta toojih karshekani chiniha," [Sanchi Disaster from Beginning until Justification for Chinese Obstruction] *Arman Daily*, January 15, 2018, p. 1; and "Daryanavardan pas az hadeseh zendeh poodand," [Sailors were Alive after Incident] *Aftab Yazd*, January 16, 2018; pp. 1, 3.
145 "Sanchi Sinking Could be 'Worst Situation' for Marine Ecology: Experts," *Global Times*, January 14, 2018; and "'Sanchi' ganj sookhteh," ['Sanchi', Burnt Treasure] *Ebtekar*, January 27, 2018, pp. 1, 5.
146 "Price Protests Turn Political as Rallies Spread," *Reuters*, December 29, 2017; "Protests over Alleged Corruption and Rising Prices Spread to Tehran," *The Guardian*, December 30, 2017; and "Iran Deploys Revolutionary Guards to Quell 'Sedition' in Protest Hotbeds," *Reuters*, January 3, 2018.
147 "Asrar Sanchi: Afkar omoomi montazer pasokhi baray shayeat marboot be naftkesh irani hastand," [Sanchi Mysteries: Public Opinions Waiting Response about

CHAPTER 2. A GRAVY TRAIN NEVER TO GET OFF: ECONOMIC AND
FINANCIAL SPOILS

From the Ground Up

The Koreans knew very little about the Middle East when they first set
foot there in modern times. They also could find very few ready-made economic opportunities that might help improve their own poor economic circumstances at home. They had to scramble to find a way to import some of
the region's raw materials, oil in particular.

That situation changed in the early 1970s, when the oil shock and the
ensuing business bonanza brought about a seismic change in the Korean
economic relationship with the Middle East and especially the Persian Gulf
region. As more petrodollars flew to the coffers of wealthy oil states in the region, more development plans and larger construction projects were carved
out. The region suddenly became a rendezvous for Western and Eastern
companies which seemingly had all the finance and expertise they needed to
take on a wide range of lucrative projects. As latecomers with little expertise
and experience in the region, Koreans could not immediately snatch up large
and bankable opportunities.[148]

Rumors Related to the Iranian Oil Tanker] *Ghanoon Daily*, January 16, 2018, pp. 1, 11;
and "Modiramel sherkat melli naftkesh azl shod/pay fajeeh 'Sanchi' dar myan ast?"
[CEO of National Tanker Company is discharged/Is 'Sanchi' Disaster Playing a Role?]
Tabnak, March 5, 2018.
148 "The Koreans Are Coming! The Koreans Are Coming!" *Engineering News-Record*,
Vol. 198, No. 13 (1977), p. 16.

They first had little option to work independently, but they managed to get started by hiring themselves out to the experienced and highly capitalized companies, especially American and Japanese ones, in order to hone their skills and get to know the nuts and bolts of working in a Middle Eastern environment. By starting primarily as subcontractors for foreign companies and taking on rather cheap and less challenging construction projects, Koreans managed to emerge later as major competitors in the market; eventually they were bold enough to engage in one-upmanship with those Western and Eastern contractors which had assisted them earlier on.

Besides some important lessons gleaned from the construction projects of the post-Korean War and post-Vietnam periods, an ace in the hole for Koreans was the relatively cheap and hardworking indentured laborers who had been supplied directly from the ROK. Although some Koreans workers were also hired by foreign companies active in the region, an overwhelming majority of them had been assembled by the Korean government and dispatched there to toil and moil for the interests of Korean contractors.[149]

A decade earlier, South Korea had sent miners and hospital nurses to West Germany in line with its "Treaty of Mutual Cooperation" with the German government. A prime motive for the ROK in such a decision was to get rid of its surplus workforce at home. But a more compelling reason was to exchange its manpower for the badly-needed foreign currency when the East Asian country was in the throes of financial difficulties; this influx of cash helped to underwrite its newly planned development and industrialization projects.[150]

The United States and Japan had partly financed some of Korea's ambitious projects, but the government itself had to come up with new plans to generate sufficient foreign exchange to fund dozens of ambitious industrialization plans. In particular, establishing a number of strategic heavy industries required major investment, while many other economic projects in the ROK also required financing and foreign equipment which could not be

---

149 "The East-West Battle," *Financial Times*, January 22, 1979; and "All Eyes on the Generals," *Middle East Economic Digest (MEED)*, April 1983, pp. 43–65.
150 "Overseas Construction Deals Surpass $60 Billion," *Chosun Ilbo*, November 15, 2010; "Korean Builders See Boon from Arab Spring," *Chosun Ilbo*, May 27, 2011; "Korea's Overseas Construction Orders Top $15 Billion in First Two Months this Year," *Arirang News*, March 21, 2014; and "17% of Middle East Wealth Builders Invest in Real Estate: Citi," *Daily News Egypt*, March 29, 2015.

covered by the weak domestic budget or by various loans and grants coming from other countries.[151]

Unlike the experience of Western Germany, however, the post-oil shock boom in the Persian Gulf led to the creation of a colossal construction market that lasted for about one and half decades, and it never did dwindle down to a trickle.[152] Over the course of that fortuitous period, more than one million indentured Korean workers as well as hundreds of their companies went to the region so that the huge earnings they made could greatly and timely assist their home country.

Although Saudi Arabia turned out to be, by and large, their prime destination and largest market, other countries in the region such as Iran were not at all immune to their penetration. As late as May 1977, some 3,000 Koreans were working in Iran and their presence hardly came to a total halt even in the heydays of the Iran–Iraq War. Over a period of just one decade from 1975 to 1985, for instance, more than 25,000 Koreans found a chance to work in Iran in spite of the Iranian government's apparent reluctance to offer domestic job opportunities to foreign nationals.[153]

The Iranian environment provided them with invaluable experiences, some of which were pivotal in South Korea's long-term connections to the Persian Gulf. From hard politics to soft culture, Koreans needed this opportunity to learn about things in Iran from scratch, now that they had earmarked the country as a major market in the region in long run. The overall situation in Iran was rather favorable to Koreans. Not only was the climate in Iran far more appealing than the sweltering weather in the Arab countries located in the southern part of the Persian Gulf, but for many Koreans the Persian language was easier to pick up. Some of those Koreans, or their children and relatives, could later engage in direct business activities with Iran

151 "Support Center Planned for Korean Builders in Middle East," *Chosun Ilbo*, July 20, 2011; "Hyundai Engineering Exceeds $80 Billion in Overseas Orders," *Chosun Ilbo*, August 5, 2011; "Overseas Construction Orders Won by S. Korean Builders up 35 pct in 2014," *Yonhap News Agency*, June 2, 2014; and "Korea's Daelim Building Town Near Tehran," *Press TV*, October 12, 2015.

152 "Korea No. 7 in Int'l Construction Market Last Year," *Chosun Ilbo*, September 8, 2011; "S Korean Builders' Mideast Success Hurts," *Financial Times*, January 5, 2014; "Will Thawing Sanctions against Iran Boost Construction Business?" *Dong-A Ilbo*, February 3, 2014; and "Big Korean Builder Sends All New Staff Abroad," *Chosun Ilbo*, April 24, 2015.

153 Shirzad Azad, *Koreans in the Persian Gulf: Policies and International Relations* (Abingdon and New York: Routledge, 2015), p. 84.

by taking advantage of their previous experiences in the country. And this is one important reason why Koreans ended up quite pleased, if quietly so, about their ultimate business record in Iran.

Balance of Trade — Aside from Oil

The experts who carved out the early plans for industrialization and development in the ROK also shaped the attitudes of the politicians and administrators who were to implement those schemes and ideas. Regardless of their education and ideological orientation, those often-unknown specialists and professionals instilled in the minds of top officials certain beliefs and convictions which were to significantly influence the basic logic and methods of managing South Korea's domestic and foreign affairs. This subtle influence was very critical when major affairs of state had to be run by a bunch of military men in civilian clothes who themselves possessed relatively little expertise in critical areas under their control.[154] Even if some of them, like Park Chung-hee, had already got some education and experience in Japan, they still desperately needed ideas and advice from advisors, be they Koreans or foreigners.

One big problem was that the state could hardly find the experts needed in every area. Because of the country's exports-oriented industrialization and development strategies, this shortcoming was more obvious in the realm of foreign policy which was now coming to the fore. Instruction manuals and policy reports could not cover everything, while quick solutions and real answers were far from clear on some exigent matters and unpredictable developments.[155] As a result, miscalculations and mishaps were very common even though the officials studiously sought to avoid committing any blunders for the sake of their own country's national interests. Other problems occurred when there was a difference of opinion or when contradictory objectives were identified in their critical relationship with other regions.

With regard to the Mideast and especially the wealthy oil-producing countries, many Korean elites had essentially developed the view that those

154 Peter D. Hershock and Roger T. Ames, eds., *Confucian Cultures of Authority* (Albany, NY: State University of New York Press, 2006); and Iain Pirie, *The Korean Developmental State: From Dirigisme to Neo-liberalism* (Abingdon and New York: Routledge, 2008), p. 60.
155 Daniel A. Bell, *Beyond Liberal Democracy: Political Thinking for an East Asian Context* (Princeton, NJ: Princeton University Press, 2006), p. 89.

"lucky" states had been presented their precious black gold on a silver platter without having to struggle to generate hard capital the way others had to do. Some powerful and influential Koreans were even tempted to disregard entirely the value of oil in the international commerce of those Middle East countries blessed with that crude fortune.[156] Of course, it can create hard feelings when one nation apparently finds wealth right under its feet and another nation has to fight tooth and nail to earn its livelihood. Korea had to work hard and smart to get any cash at all; their counterparts in the Middle East could generate plenty of capital at the drop of a hat. As compared to the way wealthy oil countries were governed, moreover, Korean managers of early industrialization and development programs had the impression that they themselves were doing something really exceptional, though a great deal of their "extraordinary" performance was patched together from American technology and Japanese finance, with Koreans themselves mainly in charge of less demanding assembly-line work.[157]

Whether or not the imprudent sentiment of those Koreans toward the Middle Eastern oil was out of ignorance or covetousness, a great deal of their recent economic activities and industrialization projects badly depended on the crude supplied by this or other Mideast country. But here was the crux of the problem; on one side, Koreans tended to rather belittle and disparage the role of oil in the foreign trade of the petroleum-exporting countries and, on the other side, they were always scoffing at their own country's growing trade deficit with those states largely because of the critically required crude supplied by them. And still worse was that they almost always used such a trade deficit as a bargaining chip in their bilateral negotiations with oil-exporting countries in order to convince them to give a better deal to Koreans. Whenever talks were held over a political issue or an economic project, the Korean negotiators would use the trade deficit as an argument for pushing for better terms. And the Koreans were generally more successful in Iran than in other oil-producing countries in the greater Middle East.[158]

---

156 Such strange thinking can be found, for instance, in Park Chong-hee's book. For more details, see: Chung-hee Park, *Kunggawa hydngmydngiwa na* [The Country, the Revolution, and I] (Seoul: Hyangmunsa, 1963).

157 Pirie, pp. 67, 79.

158 "Kore az bazar milyardi Iran del mikanad?" [Will Korea Give up the Bankable Market of Iran?] *Tabnak*, June 29, 2012; and "Koreye jenoobi negaran chinishodan ba-

Even in the heydays of their construction bonanza in Saudi Arabia in the first half of the 1980s, Koreans hardly could achieve a satisfactory trade balance there. But unlike Sadia Arabia or other Arab countries, South Korea did not experience shocking trade imbalances with Iran. Quite to the contrary, there were various occasions when Korea even scored some trade surplus in its bilateral commercial interactions with the Persian Gulf country.

Iran was the largest exports market for Korean manufactured products in the entire Mideast region; it imposed little tariffs on the commodities imported, either directly or indirectly, from the ROK, and it was rather generous in various economic agreements signed with Korean delegations over the years.[159] But as more time elapsed, some truly turbulent developments and bitter experiences proved that Arab oil-producing countries in the region had treated Koreans with more sophistication and prudence than some Iranian officials during the reign of the Pahlavi monarchy.

The Ssangyang Swag: Presage to a Precarious Partnership

With the fall of the Pahlavi dynasty and before the eventual ascendancy of the Islamic Republic, Iran had to go through a period of chaos and uncertainty. Confusion and disorganization seemed to be the order of the day, with the potential to weaken Iran as a unified sovereign state. As the upheaval and disruption of normal affairs continued for some time, the dismal situation stirred up a number of centrifugal forces which unabashedly intensified their dubious and murky activities. For a large and populous country like Iran, passionate assertions of rights, of distinctions within the populace, of particular interests rather than national interests, were calamitous, endangering both the citizenry's sense of collective identity and the state's territorial integrity.

In the same way, the most demanding positions of Iranian administrative and bureaucratic affairs fell into the hands of neophytes who possessed little, if any, expertise in the area they were going to preside over. Of course, many of those new officials were well-meaning people who wished to completely overhaul the system. But a lack of appropriate skills or sufficient background about their new role would take its toll. When their responsibility and au-

zar Iran," [South Korea Worried about Chinization of Iran Market] *Tabnak*, January 24, 2016.
159 "Korea–Iran Pact Set on Insurance Dues," *Korea Times*, March 6, 1977, p. 1.

thority had something to do with the domestic affairs of the state, at least some errors could be rectified during a period of trial and error. The problem was more chronic and more often detrimental when they had to deal with a foreign country.

Many foreign countries sought to make the most of the instability in Iran. A number of Western countries took a lion's share of the country's first-rate financial assets and helped themselves to a demographic windfall as well by opening their borders to educated and well-to-do Iranians; members of the elites could simply buy a flight ticket and leave.[160]

But some of those countries did not stop there; they ruthlessly took advantage of the turmoil and backtracked on their commitments and accords, some of which had already been duly signed and even partially implemented. Countries in the East could also be tempted to pick up such behaviors and manners because they had found a very good chance to easily walk away unscathed from their pledges and obligations to a new Iran. One emblematic example was the Japanese Mitsui which decided out of the blue to permanently terminate its partnership in the Iran–Japan Petrochemical Complex (IJPC) project ostensibly for economic reasons. One other opportunist was South Korea's Ssangyang.

Under the Shah, Iran had engaged in a number of joint economic activities with the ROK one of which was a 50–50 joint refining venture between the National Iranian Oil Corporation (NIOC) and the South Korean Ssangyang Corporation. The NIOC had already paid its full share of a project which was initially supposed to consist of a $200 million oil refinery.[161] On the cusp of the Pahlavi's fall from power, however, the South Korean government had unexpectedly decided to nationalize foreign-held equity in joint refining ventures in the ROK. The South Korean government was adamantly after its nationalization policy, and the NIOC could not really resist the pertinent pressures for long. As soon as the NIOC agreed to sell its equity to Ssangyang Corporation in 1980, the Korean government offered Ssangyang enough capital to easily gain full control of the whole joint venture. After several rounds

---

160 "Iran's Brain Drain Is the West's Gain," *Bloomberg*, May 8, 2014; "U.S. Is Prime Destination for Iran's International Mail," *Radio Zamaneh*, January 20, 2015; "Tahsil 10 hezar daneshjooy irani dar America," [10,000 Iranian Students Study in the United States] *Tabnak*, February 15, 2016; and "U.S. Tech without Iranian Immigrants: No eBay, Oracle, Google, DropBox, Tinder," *VentureBeat*, January 30, 2017.

161 "Korea, Iran to Build $160 Mil Oil Refinery," *Korea Times*, October 14, 1975, p. 1.

of negotiating and bargaining between official representatives from the two parties, nevertheless, Ssangyang agreed to pay to the NIOC only a cheap sum of $20 million for its 50 percent stake in the joint project.[162]

It is still not clear how the Ssangyang case could influence the mentality of Iranian officials about doing business with Koreans.[163] Nor much is obvious whether the experience could actually play a role in the decision of the newly established Islamic Republic to for now maintain limited official interactions with South Korea. And while the outcome from the deal with the Korean company was not very pressing as compared to the billions of dollars of Iranian assets withheld by the West under various flawed pretexts, still it deserved some serious thought and study to find out how much the case could subsequently have a corrosive impact on the way many Korean companies, from both private and public sectors, conducted their businesses in Iran under the Islamic Republic. In the heydays of crippling sanctions levied against Iran during the presidency of Ahmadinejad, for instance, many Iranian customers were heard on multiple occasions to complain about misbehaviors of Korean companies and a willingness among them to easily shun away from their commitments and obligations by taking advantage of the special circumstances Iran was going through because of the nuclear controversy.[164]

The Era Of Reconstruction And Reforms: The "Look-East" Policy

With the conclusion of the disastrous Iran–Iraq War, the Iranian government embarked on an ambitious project of reconstruction under the leadership of Akbar Hashemi Rafsanjani who had just been given the very powerful portfolio of presidency. The objective was to restore the war-damaged infrastructure and inject new life into the dilapidated situation of the Iranian economy in both micro and macro levels. In order to successfully implement the relevant programs, however, the country had to first take care of

162 The Financial Times, *Financial Times Oil and Gas International Year Book* (London: Longman, 1983), p. 481.
163 "Iranian Firm Files Claim against Korea over Failed Deal," *Korea Times*, September 22, 2015; "Iran to Invest in S. Korea as Sanctions Lifted," *KBS World Radio*, January 16, 2016; "Korea Mulls Allowing Iranian Fund to Invest in Korean Stocks," *Korea Herald*, February 3, 2016; and "Iran's Investment Plan in Osong Biotech City Likely to Gain Pace," *Yonhap News Agency*, May 4, 2016.
164 "Mamouriat gostardeh koreiha dar sarzamin forsatha," [The Broad Mission of Koreans in the Land of Opportunities] *Taadol*, May 2, 2016, p. 2; and "Farday ravabet tejari va eghtesadi Iran–koreye jenoobi," [The Future of Iran–South Korea Trade and Economic Relations] *Rah Mardom Daily*, May 3, 2016, p. 15.

various financial and technological requirements. Part of such essential pre-conditions could be obtained from abroad at some cost, but not everything was still easily and freely accessible to Iran. A number of war-time international sanctions and restrictions against Iran had remained intact, while the country was to only come under further external pressures and hurtful constraints according to the draconian diktats of "dual containment policy" and a host of other strategically and politically-oriented designs at the cost of Iran and Iranians.[165]

Following the two-term government of Rafsanjani over a course of eight years, the helm of Iranian presidency was given to Mohammad Khatami who, like his predecessor, vowed to carry on the reconstruction agenda. But his two-term tenure was to be remembered more for stoking up hot-button issues like political reforms, as a perennial bone of contention in the society, rather than engaging in any substantial infrastructure reconstruction and economic development. Because of the nature of his electoral promises and political mottos, nevertheless, Khatami came under mountainous domestic pressures, though he was never as powerful and stouthearted as Rafsanjani in the first place. Externally, the Khatami government did not encounter less pressures and constraints at all. As part of his presidency coincided with the Bush administration in the United States and the follow-up American wars in Afghanistan and Iraq, stakes became even higher for the Iranian foreign policy with Tehran itself at the crosshairs of interminable Western suspicion and intimidation.[166] In such an uncompromising and often hostile external environment, how then Rafsanjani and Khatami could look after the Persian Gulf country's growing economic needs and technological necessities.

For both governments, a simple expedient yet prudent strategy was to court a number of East Asian countries for replenishing Iran's requirements in what was to be later known as the "Look-East" orientation. As a matter of fact, this policy was in a way an extension of Iran's previous recourse to both North Korea and China for military equipment during the Iran–Iraq War period. But this time, the "Look-East" approach was essentially economic in

165 Steven Wright, *The United States and Persian Gulf Security: The Foundations of the War on Terror* (Reading, Berkshire: Ithaca Press, 2007), pp. 94–96, 189–191.
166 Jackson and Towle, p. 47.

nature, though political and even cultural elements were not absent at all.[167] In doing so, Iran also virtually became one of the first countries in the world which paid early attention to the East long before that a flurry of other nations found closer ties to Eastern countries as a good remedy for their various economic and technical demands. Although the off-hands foreign policy of Eastern nations, as compared to Western countries, was enough attractive to the Iranian governments of Rafsanjani and Khatami, nevertheless, accessibility and affordability were from the beginning a prime motivation behind Tehran's well-timed attention to the East.

The Iranian "Look-East" approach still did not imply that the country was to give equal consideration to all East Asian countries. Tehran became relatively selective in choosing its economic and technological partners from the East so that under Rafsanjani Japan and to some extent Taiwan were preferentially given a bigger role in Iran's early quest for obtaining its increasing economic and technological requirements. During the presidency of Khatami, the presence of South Korea gradually became more visible in Iran's overall economic interactions with East Asia. Although China was slowly moving to position itself as an important partner in Tehran's connections to the East under both Rafsanjani and Khatami, Beijing still had to wait for some time before becoming Iran's top trading partner, which it did during the presidency of Ahmadinejad. South Korea eventually emerged as the dark horse of Tehran's recent approach under the "Look-East" banner.

On the cusp of the new millennium, therefore, the ROK essentially became one of Iran's top trading partners so that it could soon capture some 5 percent of the Iranian markets. Within a few years, the East Asian country ratcheted up its presence in Iran by emerging as the second biggest foreign investor in Iran after Germany.[168] It was a time when Iran had turned out to become the sixth largest market for the ROK's overseas construction contractors. The "Look-East" approach was certainly contributing greatly to

---

167 "Jahangiri: Dolat ghabl 700 milyard dollar sarf eshteghal dar chin kar," [Jahangiri: Former Government Spent $700 Billion on Creating Employment in China] *Tabnak*, April 25, 2015; "Dolat Rouhani record varedat dar 100 sal akhir ra shekast," [Rouhani Government Broke the Record of Imports for the Past 100 Years] *Jahan News*, February 9, 2016; and "For Economic Revival, Iran will do a Balancing Act between East and West," *Asia Times*, March 8, 2016.

168 "Iran to Emerge the Biggest Export Market," *Business Korea*, November 8, 2004; and "Payan tejarat yektarafeh be koreye jenoobi," [End of One-way Trade with South Korea] *Donya-e Eqtesad*, March 1, 2016.

South Korea's recent achievements in Iran, but a number of other equally important internal and external elements were also paving the ground for Koreans to deepen their market penetration into Iran. Even a simple taxation policy introduced by the Iranian government had really a huge potential to bring lots of cash to the coffers of Korean companies in one way to another.[169] Among all those domestic and foreign factors instrumental in the ROK's un-expected surge in Iran, however, no factor was probably more pivotal than the role of sundry sanctions which were levied against Iran under the pretext of nuclear controversy during the presidency of Ahmadinejad.

The Crippling Sanctions: When Free Trade Becomes Forced Trade

The modern regime of Iran sanctions started principally in the wake of the infamous "hostage crisis" in 1980. Once the hostage calamity was settled and Iran agreed to free the American "diplomats" after some 444 days, the US-led West still had an axe to grind to keep in place the sanctions through-out the Iran–Iraq War.[170] The conclusion of the bloody conflict, however, did not bring to an end various injurious sanctions imposed against Iranians prior to or during the war period. Quite to the contrary, the United States in particular initiated, in line with its "dual containment policy" and other similar strategies in the Middle East and especially the Persian Gulf region, a slew of additional sanctions against Tehran — this time under new perplex-ing pretexts such as "terrorism," "human rights violations," "intervention-ism," "expansionism," and so on and so forth. Iran was already in a penalty box, and the main objective of such pernicious penalties was to keep the country on tenterhooks by denying it all sorts of required and useful resourc-es to develop and catch up.[171]

With regard to the ongoing regime of sanctions, the melodramatic two-term presidency of Ahmadinejad upped the ante. Besides his own obstrep-erous personality and contentious statements, the Iranian nuclear program now became a fortuitously fresh justification, giving the US-led West a better

---

169 "South Korea, Iran Sign Double Taxation Avoidance Agreement," *Yonhap News Agency*, January 29, 2002.
170 Alan P. Dobson, *US Economic Statecraft for Survival 1933–1991: Of Sanctions, Embargoes and Economic Warfare* (London and New York: Routledge, 2002), p. 229.
171 Robert Eyler, *Economic Sanctions: International Policy and Political Economy at Work* (New York: Palgrave Macmillan, 2007), pp. 184–186; and Kern Alexander, *Economic Sanctions: Law and Public Policy* (New York: Palgrave Macmillan, 2009), pp. 267–277.

excuse to comfortably rally the world's public opinions against Iran. Terribly lost its moral high ground in Iraq, the United States skillfully took advantage of the situation to divert attentions from its Iraqi quagmire by magnifying potential perils stemming from the Iranian nuclear program. In order to better aggrandize the nuclear issue, one potent policy was to essentially impose a more comprehensive regime of international sanctions against Iran.[172] This load of broad sanctions were to substantially target almost every aspect of Iran's international trade as well as any functional area of international interactions between the Iranians and the outside world. But since Iran was powerful and porous enough to be totally locked up, and because there happened to be perpetually strong voices even among close US allies against the new regime of sanctions, some exceptions needed to be made.[173]

The Obama administration started issuing executive decrees, excluding some countries from any financial and technological punishments for doing business with Iran as usual. Those countries included China and dozens of other states, almost all of which were America's close allies. The primary rationale was that these countries were cooperating with Washington in different ways regarding the Iranian nuclear issue, such as reducing their oil imports from the Persian Gulf country.[174] Such US interference with international trade seemed strange, and the whole matter raised suspicions that some kind of *quid pro quo* agreement had been arranged between the United States and its allies — and rivals. Still, in that exclusive list, which was regu-

---

172 "Don't Let Iran off the Hook," *Sentinel & Enterprise*, January 21, 2015; "Uncle Sam: Anti-terror Leader or Terrorist Breeder?" *Xinhua*, February 17, 2015; and "'Western Media Attempting to Portray Iran as Threat'", *Russia Today*, December 31, 2015.
173 "S. Korea, Iran Relations Face Difficulties: Envoy," *Korea Herald*, August 7, 2010; "Korea's Mark on an Expectation–Defying Iran," *Korea Herald*, August 10, 2011; "Trade Ban on Iran: Korea Allows for Intermediary Trade of 'Humanitarian' Items with Iran," *Business Korea*, October 17, 2013; "Iran's Slide to the Bottom," *Asia Times*, September 15, 2010; and "Iran's Political Economy Under and After the Sanctions," *Washington Post*, April 23, 2015.
174 "U.S. Extends Iran Oil Sanctions Waivers to China, India, South Korea," *Reuters*, November 29, 2013; "Asia is Purchasing Nearly all of Iran's Oil, *The Diplomat*, January 5, 2013; "Iran Slashes Oil Prices to Asia," *Dow Jones Newswires*, October 10, 2014; "Koreans to Raise Iran Oil, Condensate Inflows," *Press TV*, September 19, 2015; "K-sure to Support Exports to Iran," *Korea Times*, February 16, 2016; "Korean Firms Bank on Past Loyalty to Iran," *Korea Joongang Daily*, April 29, 2016; and "Asia Receives over 60% of Iran's Crude Exports," *Mehr News Agency*, October 16, 2016.

larly updated by the US State Department, no country emerged more trium-phant than South Korea, though China had its own story as well.[175]

On one side, the ROK was a bosom buddy of the United States and a bona fide backer of Washington's policies about various thorny Middle Eastern problems such as the Iranian nuclear controversy. As a matter of fact, South Korea was willing to throw its unconditional support behind the United States in the wider Middle East. Seoul had proved for decades that it had little, if any, disagreement with Washington's underlying strategic and politico-economic designs for the region.[176] That is why the ROK could both endorse various Iran-related punitive sanctions in the UN Security Coun-cil and implement them soon after, no matter how much Koreans scoffed at those ill-timed measures among themselves privately. The only agonizing matter was how to avoid or minimize the potentially huge cost those policies could incur, as they ran counter to the growing interests of Korean compa-nies in Iran. Since their preoccupation was to either partially or even wholly compensate for that loss, the Obama administration's successive executive decrees providing an exception were quite welcome.[177]

On the other side, the more the East Asian state adhered to the sanctions diktats levied against Iran, the closer the two countries grew economically, and even culturally. Regardless of Seoul's initial political concessions given (rather quietly) to those measures, the trade turnover between the two par-ties went up year after year, as if they were simply experiencing the healthy growth of normal interactions. To the surprise of many, the peak of Iran sanctions paradoxically marked the pinnacle of commercial interactions be-tween South Korea and Iran.[178] This was no mere quirk of fate nor was it a be-

175 Shirzad Azad, "Principlism Engages Pragmatism: Iran's Relations with East Asia under Ahmadinejad," *Asian Politics & Policy*, Vol. 7, No. 4 (October 2015), pp. 555–573.
176 "Korea Takes Tougher Stance on Iran," *Korea Joongang Daily*, December 17, 2011; "S. Korea Holds Celebration of Prodemocracy Movement amid Boycott," *Yonhap News Agency*, May 18, 2014; "Korea, US in Dialogue over NK, Iran," *Korea Times*, August 21, 2014; "With Iran's Return, N.K. Conundrum Only Set to Deepen," *Korea Herald*, January 17, 2016; and "Tehran, Seoul Must Resist US Malice in Ties: Leader," *Press TV*, May 2, 2016.
177 "Seoul to be Exempted in Some Part of Iran Sanction," *Korea Joongang Daily*, February 20, 2012.
178 "5 keshvar bozorg saderkonandeh kala be Iran," [5 Largest Exporters of Commodity to Iran] *Asr Iran*, February 21, 2016; "With Sanctions Lifted, South Korea Eyes Investment Links to Iran," *World Politics Review*, May 16, 2016; "Iran–South Korea Export Jumps for 10 Times," *Trend News Agency*, May 30, 2016; and "Korean Delegates in Iran to Expand Market," *Korea Herald*, August 5, 2016.

wildering game. Still, Obama's exceptional decrees could not contribute so greatly to the ROK's expanding presence in Iran in the midst of all-embracing and exhaustive economic and financial measures implemented against Iran during the Ahmadinejad presidency. What else then could have been boosting South Korea's clout in the Persian Gulf country under those peculiar circumstances?

One Stone Two Birds: The Blocked Funds

Like the sanctions, the story of frozen funds essentially dates back to the time of the "hostage crisis." The US government exploited that crisis by seizing billions of dollars in Iranian assets in the United States. And the Americans refused to release them, even after the crisis was resolved.

The asset seizure was particularly harmful at a time when Iran needed resources for its growing military requirements.[179]While there are no exact official figures on this issue, and estimates vary, the real value of Iran's frozen assets in the United States was between $10 and $24 billion, including $1.973 billion of frozen assets and $50 million of the estimated value of real estate and their accumulated/accrued rent.

Later, successive governments in the Islamic Republic had little to worry about similar steps by one or another American administration simply because Iran was not engaged much in economic exchanges with the United States. But Iran had simultaneously established various important economic and financial connections to many American allies and friends around the world, Europe in particular. Iranian assets in these countries were, therefore, always an innocent target of any potential move by Washington against Tehran.[180]

New innovations and technological improvements, in particular, increased the American sway over the Iranian assets abroad over time. Moreover, the US economic and financial systems gradually and significantly expanded their influence, if not say their power and control, over both ways and means of doing business in many other parts of the world. The coming

---

179 David R. Farber, *Taken Hostage: The Iran Hostage Crisis and America's First Encounter with Radical Islam* (Princeton, NJ: Princeton University Press, 2005), p. 119; and David Patrick Houghton, *US Foreign Policy and the Iran Hostage Crisis* (New York: Cambridge University Press, 2004), p. 46–50.
180 "The Master Plan to Manage Iran: Keep Containing It," *The National Interest*, December 2, 2014.

age of internet and mass communications was to only consolidate the American authority in such areas. As more electronic money became a norm in conducting international business, and as Iran revved up both the volume and value of its economic and financial exchanges with close US allies in different regions, the more Tehran was to become vulnerable to any Western ransom over its funds and resources kept somewhere abroad. By the time the new round of crippling comprehensive sanctions were carved out against Iran under Ahmadinejad, therefore, the country was already holding huge assets abroad, ranging from foreign currency reserves to crude revenues. But since it was neither plausible nor economically viable to transfer all such assets to safe places in the run-up to the implementation of sanctions, a great amount of them had to be ineluctably blocked in different parts of the world, including South Korea.[181]

In line with its pugnacious policy of sanctions circumvention, the Ahmadinejad government strived hard to get part, if not all, of those blocked assets released — or at least to prevent further problems of that kind. The notorious quest eventually led to the creation of a colossal black market economy which straddled all five continents.[182] Iranians were not willing to easily give up their inalienable rights, and such tenacity had to ultimately ruin one group and corrupt another one. Later, during the presidency of Rouhani a number of scandals were exposed, giving credence to some speculations that Tehran's varied strategies to bypass the sanctions had corrupted many people both inside and outside the country. In another case, and equally abysmal, it was revealed that the Chinese government had tried to take advantage of the situation, bludgeoning the Iranian government into an undesirable deal

---

181 "Iranian MP: Some $60 Billion Worth of Iran Assets Blocked by Foreign Banks," *Trend News Agency*, August 2, 2013; "Japanese, S. Korean, Swiss Banks to Transfer Iran's Frozen Money," *Fars News Agency*, January 28, 2014; "South Korea Set to Make Oil Payment to Iran – Source," *Reuters*, February 12, 2014; "Iran's $300 Billion Shakedown," *Foreign Policy*, April 16, 2015; "$8.8 Billion Iran Money Blocked in India," *Press TV*, May 16, 2015; "S. Korean Bank to Finance $5 Billion Projects in Iran," *Tehran Times*, September 8, 2015; and "South Korea, Iran to Keep won-based Settlement System," *Korea Times*, February 2, 2016.

182 "Two Montreal Men Charges for Exporting Railway Equipment to Iran," *Montreal Gazette*, October 13, 2015; and "'State-of-the-art' Subterfuge: How Iran Kept Flying under Sanctions," *Reuters*, January 31, 2016.

with regard to some of the funds which Tehran had transferred from Europe to Beijing in order to save them from this or that sanctions laws.[183]

In South Korea, the Iranian funds blocked under various sanctions regulations were estimated to be around $5 billion, if not more. Considering the fact that the South Korean government had to beg Saudi Arabia to deposit some $500 million of its oil money in Seoul in the aftermath of the first oil shock, the $5 billion blocked Iranian oil funds in the ROK was a lot of dough to be left to the Koreans without even interest being accrued.[184] Of course, both the Iranian and Korean governments had already made some arrangements to facilitate their economic and financial interactions both prior to and in the middle of sanctions implementation. Such measures, including the creation of an *ad hoc* branch by an Iranian bank in Seoul, still could not give Iran easy and timely access to all of its oil revenues in the East Asian country.[185] Not only that banking branch had to be ultimately shut down because of the new sanctions laws, Tehran became even more vulnerable with regards to its assets in Seoul over time because it could supply crude to the ROK but did not have the permission to return back the pertinent revenues.[186]

On top of that, the Korean government was stubborn in pushing the sanctions regulations down the throat of its companies from both public and private sectors which were doing business with Iran. This could make it even harder for some concerned people in Iran to counteract the sanctions measures implemented by Koreans or find new creative ways, similar to some steps taken in different parts of the world then, to release their coun-

183 "Goftogoo ba Tahmasb Mazaherin dar mored arzhay bloukeshode," [Dialogue with Tahmasb Mazaheri on Blocked Funds] *Shargh Daily*, July 25, 2015, p. 1; and "Tahmasb Mazaherin: Gharadadhay 'shebh Turkmenchay' ba chin badtar az blokeshodan amval bood," [Tahmasb Mazaherin: 'Turkmenchai-style' Contracts with China Were Worse Than Blocked Properties] *Asr Iran*, August 9, 2015.

184 "Billions of Iranian Petrodollars Blocked by South Korea," *Trend News Agency*, October 22, 2014; and "Iran May Clear Its Funds Out of 2 Korean Banks," *Korea Joongang Daily*, January 29, 2016.

185 "South Korea to Close Iranian Bank Branch," *Wall Street Journal*, September 8, 2010; "Lesson of an Iran Sanctions Saga in Seoul," *Forbes*, March 24, 2015; and "Iran's Mellat Bank to Reopen Seoul Branch Next Month," *Korea Herald*, February 24, 2016.

186 "Iran Sanctions Eased, Relief for S. Korean Economy," *Yonhap News Agency*, January 20, 2014; "Korean Bourse Operator Signs MOU with Iran," *Yonhap News Agency*, October 23, 2015; "Eximbank Chief Eyes Iranian Market," *Korea Times*, January 25, 2016; "S. Korea in Final Stages of Preparations to Trade with Iran in Euro," *Reuters*, August 3, 2016; and "Iran's Bank Sepah to Open Branches in China, South Korea," *Trend News Agency*, November 4, 2016.

try's seized funds in the ROK. The only alternative was, therefore, to keep supplying oil to South Korea and bringing back part of the revenues in the form of imported goods from this or other Korean company. The oil money in Seoul was big enough, and the thirst of Iranian bustling markets for Korean products insatiable.[187] This approach, along with a number of other policies and practices, led to the widespread appearance of Korean commodities in Iran as other more sought-after brands were temporarily withdrawn.

Mortgaged Markets: The Omnipresence Of Korean Brands

A large presence of foreign products in Iran is not really a new phenomenon. It started at least as far back as the 1970s, when the first oil shock enabled the country to import various commodities, consumer products in particular, from Western countries on a grand scale.

In the 1980s and early 1990s, Japanese brands started making inroads into Iranian markets, but their presence waned again once the bubble burst in Japan. But even during their halcyon days in Iran, the actual presence and visibility of Japanese products in Iran did not compare to what is now widely seen with regard to various Korean brands.[188] In fact, it would be no exaggeration at all to claim that such omnipresence and domination of certain brands from a single country is unprecedented in Iran's history. This market penetration can be easily observed in both public and private sectors.[189]

In the public sector, many key ministries and influential organizations have moved in recent years to equip their staff with different Korean brands. It is not difficult now to observe how the entire computer system of a major public institution in Iran is supplied by desktops of only one or two Korean brands. This mind-boggling phenomenon is particularly common in top national universities around the country. The same can be easily observed with regard to lots of other items widely-used by prominent public bodies, ranging from everyday stationery to kitchen utensils and from fax machines

187 "Habs poolhay petroshimi Iran dar kore," [Blockage of Iranian Petrochemical Moneys in Korea] *Mashregh*, October 22, 2014.
188 "Kalahay ajibi ke vared Iran mishavad," [Strange Goods which are Imported into Iran] *Asr Iran*, May 17, 2015; and "Porkardan bazar az kalahay khareji baray keshvar mazyat nist," [Filling out Markets by Foreign Goods not an Advantage for the Country] *Kar va Kargar*, July 14, 2015, p. 1.
189 "Iran Attractive for S. Korean Firms: Official," *Yonhap News Agency*, September 15, 2015; "Woori Bank to Open 'Korea Desk' at Iranian Bank," *Korea Times*, March 7, 2016; and "Woori Bank Launches Service Desk in Iran," *Press TV*, May 3, 2016.

to fire extinguishers. We may add to the list the personal belongings of many officials who almost always have with them more than one Korean brand, be it their cellphone, laptop, or automobile, etc.[190] Of course, a great many of those various Korean brands are today produced in and shipped by China, but their pervasive presence in the major public institutions ineluctably entails negative implications in one way or another.[191]

The situation in the private sector and personal lives of the citizenry is far more alarming. The Korean brands have simply taken over a wide range of domestic appliances used by Iranian families, while a growing number of single and never-married youth and adults in the country are increasingly relying on Korean items.[192] There are many families whose preferred brands are now largely, if not entirely, Korean: that includes their cellphones, laptops, desktops, vacuum cleaners, irons, refrigerators, stoves, heating and cooling systems, personal automobiles, and so forth.[193] These goods are all supplied by the numerous Samsung and LG outlets which have been opened in almost every street of Iranian cities and towns. Moreover, representatives of Korean automobile companies are equally pervasive across Iran's bustling markets. That is why sometimes a long line of expensive Korean-made cars dazzles the eyes of any innocent and upright bystander in Tehran and other major cities.[194]

Based on a report published by Iran Chamber of Commerce, Industries, Mines and Agriculture, the total volume of bilateral trade between Iran and

---

190 "Hyundai Motor Group Bets Big on Middle East," *Korea Herald*, April 22, 2015; and "'Suzuki to Introduce Four Models to Iran'," *Press TV*, September 3, 2015; and "10 mazyat Iran baray kharejiha," [10 Advantages of Iran for Foreigners] *Asr Iran*, October 4, 2015.

191 "Bazar khodroohay varedati dar ekhtiyar koreiha," [Koreans Have a Hold over Iranian Market of Imported Cars] *Etemad*, June 22, 2016.

192 "Aya bazar Iran supermarket kalahay korei baghi mimanad?" [Will Iran Market Remain a Supermarket of Korean Goods?] *Iranian Students News Agency (ISNA)*, February 26, 2016.

193 "Apple in Talks to Sell iPhone in Iran," *Korea Herald*, October 30, 2014; "Jahangiri Urges Consumers to Use Domestic Goods," *Mehr News Agency*, April 25, 2015; "Iran Could be a Big Deal for Asian Manufacturers," *Bloomberg*, July 20, 2015; "Iran's Cellphone Imports Fall By 25%," *Trend News Agency*, April 13, 2016; and "Iran Auto Imports Grow 54% over," *Financial Tribune*, February 2, 2017.

194 "Amar takandahandeh varedat khodroo," [Shocking Statistics on Car Imports] *Tabnak*, September 16, 2015; "Monasebat Tehran–Seoul az negah amar," [A Statistical Look at Tehran–Seoul Interactions] *Donya-e Eqtesad*, May 1, 2016; and "Bazar khodroohay varedati Iran dar ekhtiayr koreiha," [Iranian Market of Imported Cars Captured by Koreans] *Etemad*, June 22, 2016, p. 5.

South Korea increased significantly from around $500 million in 1979 to $1.8 billion in 1997. By 2010, the two-way trade had ratcheted up to $11.5 billion before reaching its crescendo of $15.5 billion in 2011.[195] The estimated figure for 2017 was $10 billion.[196] In 2015 and 2016, the ROK was the fifth top destination for Iran's exports before moving to become the fourth destination in 2017 after China, Iraq, and the United Arab Emirates (UAE), respectively. With regard to imports, however, in the period between 2013 and 2017 South Korea maintained its critical position as the Persian Gulf country's third greatest source of imported commodities, right after China and the UAE.[197]

Of course, the foregoing trade statistics cover only those commercial interactions which are handled through recognized routes and official bodies in charge of external trade. Since the UAE produces virtually nothing besides fossil fuels, the statistics for trade between Iran and the tiny Arab state are pretty much misleading. During the presidency of Ahmadinejad, for instance, there happened to be a significant hike in the volume of Korean products imported into Iran through unofficial channels and smuggling, a great deal of it from the UAE. It is next to impossible to put any estimate on the total value of all Korean goods that entered Iran by different subterranean methods. Their universal presence throughout the Iranian markets proves that the quantity and value of Korean products far exceeds the data and statistics released by official bodies.

Korean commodities are disturbingly ubiquitous in Iran. About a decade ago, 70 percent of the TV market in Iran supplied by LG and Samsung, while 40 percent of the entire cellphone market monopolized by Samsung Mobile.[198] In a long report published in February 2010, the Korean newspaper *Dong-A Ilbo* claimed that the use of "made-in-Korean household appliances"

195 "Hajm tejarat Iran va korye jenoobi cheghadr ast?" [How Much is the Volume of Trade between Iran and South Korea?] *Iran Chamber of Commerce, Industries, Mines and Agriculture*, April 30, 2016. Some other Persian sources have given a figure of $17 billion or more for 2011 when the bilateral Iranian–South Korean trade reached its pinnacle.
196 "Hajm mobadelat tejari Iran va korye be 10 milliard dollar resid," [Volume of Trade Exchanges between Iran and Korea Reached $10 Billion] *Alalam News Network*, November 29, 2017.
197 "Chegooneh korye jenoobi sevvomin sharik tejari Iran shod?" [How Did South Korea Become Iran's Third Trade Partner?] *Tabnak*, September 12, 2017.
198 "Samsung Shares 32.4 Percent of Iran's TV Market," *Trend News Agency*, October 19, 2013; and "Taghdim dodasti bazarha be kharejiha," [Markets Offered to Foreigners on a Silver Platter] *Shargh Daily*, November 6, 2016, p. 4.

in Iran was 75 percent.[199] And it was just half a decade ago when more than 70 percent of all imported automobiles into Iran had been manufactured only by the three South Korean companies of Kia Motors, Hyundai, and the notorious Ssangyang Corporation.[200] This shocking situation has not really improved much today as a number of recent surveys report that some 40 percent of the entire furniture market in Iran is still captured by the Korean LG and Samsung companies.[201] And in spite of the signing of the nuclear deal and various fresh interactions between Iranian companies and their counterparts in other parts of the world over the past years, the three South Korean brands are still monopolizing some 60 percent of the whole market of imported automobiles and personal vehicles into Iran.[202]

The penetration of Korean products into the Persian Gulf country has even reached the less known yet up-and-coming market of cigarettes. South Korea's largest tobacco firm, for instance, Korea Tobacco & Ginseng Corporation (KT&G), has managed to capture an astonishing market share of 10 percent, after some major international rivals such as Japan Tobacco and British American Tobacco. Having entered the Iranian market in 2007, the KT&G soon concluded an agreement with Iran's state-owned tobacco maker, ITC, building its branch of KT&G Pars and setting up a factory in the capital, Tehran, in order to make Esse and Pine cigarettes.[203] The KT&G is now surprisingly the only South Korean company with an overseas branch in Iran, taking advantage of the Persian Gulf as a beachhead to spread into

---

199 "Hallyue bbajin ilan," [A Fallen for Korean Wave Iran] *Dong-A Ilbo*, February 22, 2010.
200 "Tahrime Iran tavasotte KIA shekast khord," ["Kia's Iran Embargo Failed"], *Iranian Students' News Agency (ISNA)*, September 24, 2011; and "South Korea, Iran Sign $1B Auto Deal," *Trend News Agency*, May 29, 2016.
201 "65 darsad bazar lavazm khanegi var ekhtiyar sherkathay khareji ast," [65 Percent of Furniture Market Seized by Foreign Companies] *Jahan News*, May 15, 2016; and "Lavazem khaneghi: Bazar shesh milyard dollari," [Furniture: A $6 Billion Market] *7Sobh Daily*, June 19, 2016, p. 1.
202 "Korean Auto Parts Suppliers to Benefit from Sanctions Lifting against Iran," *Korea IT Times*, January 22, 2014; "Korean Carmakers Bet on Mideast Market," *Chosun Ilbo*, April 16, 2014; "Korea's Hyundai Gains Lion Share of Iran's Car Imports Market," *Trend News Agency*, November 16, 2014; "LG Uplus to Export Smart Car Solution to Middle East," *Korea Herald*, February 23, 2015; and "LG to Develop Electric Car for Iran," *Chosun Ilbo*, May 13, 2016.
203 "Japan Tobacco Buys Iranian Cigarette Maker to Boost Dominance," *Financial Times*, October 18, 2015; "KT&G Expands Business in Iran," *The Korea Herald*, February 10, 2016; and "Hangug tambae, tongnama deung sinheung sijangseo hwallo," [Emerging Markets Such as Southeast Asia Succumb to Korean Cigarette] *Hankook Ilbo*, September 21, 2017.

the greater Middle East and other neighboring regions. While KT&S's Esse sold only $1.1 million in Iran in 2011, its sales grew by more than 2000 percent within four years, reaching to $24.7 million in 2015.[204]

The monopoly of Korean companies over the Iranian markets and their ungrateful, and sometimes hurtful, behaviors toward the Iranians once again became the focus of a heated national debate in Iran in February 2018. Samsung refused to share its giveaway special smartphones to the four Iranian athletes who were participating at the Winter Olympics held in Pyeongchang, South Korea.[205] The move, which kept the world as well as the Iranian media abuzz and was initially justified under the UN sanctions diktats embarrassed Iranian authorities both in the public and private sectors, forcing the government to immediately summon the South Korean ambassador in Tehran to the foreign ministry.[206]

Although Samsung swiftly reversed its outrageous move and made overtures to the officials who were leading the Iranian sports team for the Olympics, the die had already been cast. Befuddled and flabbergasted by the humiliating act of the Korean company, many Iranian media and press representatives were sorely furious, calling for a national boycott of Samsung products in Iran.[207] By accentuating the fact that Samsung makes $2.7 billion annually from the Iranian mobile market alone, it was a legitimate question why Iranians should be boycotted for the Olympics, but not for their lucrative market."[208] In reaction to the demeaning act of Samsung, they

204 "KT&G's Exports Exceed Sales at Home," *The Korea Herald*, January 18, 2016; "Guksan tambae, ilan sobija salojabda," [Korean Cigarette Catches up with Iranian Consumers] *Asia Kyungjae*, January 29, 2016; and "KT&G Successful in New Overseas Markets," *Korea Times*, March 16, 2016.

205 "Iran is Angry Its Athletes Weren't Offered Smartphones at the Winter Olympics and Now It's a Problem," *Business Insider*, February 8, 2018; "Samsung Smartphone Ban for Iranian Olympians!" *Financial Tribune*, February 8, 2018; and "Iranian Athletes to Receive Samsung Phones without Condition," *Yonhap News Agency*, February 9, 2018.

206 "Iran Foreign Ministry: Samsung Must Apologize for Gift Ban against Olympics Athletes," *Iran Daily*, February 8, 2018; "S Korean Envoy Summoned over Samsung Phones Scandal," *Mehr News Agency*, February 8, 2018; and "Ehzar modiran Samsung ba dastoor dadsetan kol," [Prosecutor General Summons Samsung Managers] *Tabnak*, February 9, 2018.

207 "Ilanseo 'samseong bulmae'," [Call for 'Samsung Boycott' in Iran] *Yonhap News Agency*, February 8, 2018; and "Tahrim mahsoolat Samsung kamtarin pasokh be rafter tahghiramiz korye jenoobi," [Boycotting Samsung Products Minimum Response to Humiliating Behavior of South Korea] *Kayhan*, February 8, 2018, pp. 1, 10.

208 "Koreihay soodjoo: korye jenoobi dar tejarat ba Iran be manafe yektarafeh esrar darad," [Korean Self-seekers: South Korea Insists on One-way Interests in Trade with Iran] *Shahrvand*, February 10, 2018, pp. 1, 2.

particularly suggested a number of retaliatory measures, including boycotting Samsung's products by the Iranian people and officials, putting a ban on the importation of Samsung's products, and creating serious restrictions for Samsung's activities in Iran.[209]

Across the political spectrum, moreover, pundits and observers asked the government to reconsider the whole issue of bilateral commercial ties with South Korea. Highlighting various treacherous moves taken against Iran by the Koreans during the sanctions era, they were all rather unanimous in pointing out the flawed nature and untenable prospect of trade between the two countries. In addition to the moral and emotional pain Samsung had temporarily inflicted upon the country, some other aspects of commercial relationship between Iran and the ROK have long been a contentious issue in Iran.[210]

In contrast to the ubiquity of Korean manufactured goods in Iran, for instance, South Korea still adamantly refuses to import any significant amount of Iranian goods beyond raw materials and energy resources.[211] It is actually very hard to find any trace of Iranian products in South Korea, and this unfair game of "bilateral" trade will hardly change in favor of Iran anytime soon, no matter how many new agreements and MOUs were signed between South Korean and Iranian officials in recent years.[212]

Moreover, the Iranians themselves can be partly blamed for the problem. Whether they hail from the public or private sector, many Iranians are happy to indulge their own personal interests at the cost of their country and fellow citizens by consistently purchasing and importing Korean products in large quantities. Their culpability can perhaps be encapsulated by the term of a

---

209 "Pishnahad shoma dar vakonesh be tohin Samsung be varzeshkaran Irani?" [What is Your Suggestion in Reaction to Samsung's Insult to Iranian Athletes?] *Tabnak*, February 10, 2018.

210 "Basat Samsung jameh shaved," [Kick out Samsung] *Mehr News Agency*, February 9, 2018; "Shomaresh maekoos baray tahrim Samsung dar Iran," [Countdown to Samsung Boycott in Iran] *Tejarat Online*, February 10, 2018; and "Samsung chegooneh ba Iran tejarat mikonad," [How Does Samsung Trade with Iran] *Jahan Eghtesad*, February 14, 2018.

211 "Korean Oil Companies Accelerate Efforts to Wean Themselves from Middle East," *Business Korea*, February 9, 2015; "Iran's Exports to South Korea Increases by 1400%," *Trend News Agency*, July 4, 2016; and "Korean Oil Refiners Diversifying Crude Oil Exporters," *Business Korea*, October 4, 2016.

212 "Yonhap Renews News Exchange Agreement with Iranian Counterpart," *Yonhap News Agency*, May 16, 2016.

so-called "imports mafia" and "smuggling market," phenomena which have greatly contributed to the omnipresence of Korean brands in Iran.[213]

The Imports Mafia: The Tip of the Spear

The term "imports mafia" became a leitmotiv of certain Iranian press and media outlets from the presidency of Ahmadinejad onward. The public did not necessarily understand this dubious terminology, as reports continued to remain vague and imprecise; few specific details could be revealed about major characteristics of the mafia or even what types of people were behind it. Interested individuals, however, could understand what such a *cliché* might imply. After all, the import mafia was not entirely, or even mostly, governmental and quasi-governmental; the private citizenry and individuals with no close ties to the public sector were certainly a major force behind the mafia.[214]

The import mafia was dealing with foreign products and services brought in from various other countries. As successive Iranian governments were not exclusively in charge of this crucial business, individuals and companies from the private sector inevitably had to be given a role to play, though some semi-governmental bodies and non-governmental organizations (NGOs) still deeply remained involved in this often profitable area.[215] For whatever reasons, governments offered, sometimes on a silver platter, various trade advantages and imports privileges exclusively to certain individuals, families, and institutions.[216] These favored people and privileged groups normally formed the backbone of the imports mafia throughout past decades, though some of them were not always able to perpetually benefit from their eas-

213 "Yek shakhs nimi az varedat khodroo be keshvar ra dar ekhtiyar darad," [One Person Controls Half of Car Imports into the Country] *Khabar Online*, February 3, 2015; "Har mantagheh Iran yek padeshah ghachagh darad," [Every Region in Iran Have a Smuggling King] *Tabnak*, August 24, 2015; and "Yek sevvom eghtesad Iran dast ghachaghchihast," [A Third of Iran Economy in the Hands of Smugglers] *Jahan News*, January 19, 2016.

214 Rodney Wilson, *Economic Development in the Middle East* (London and New York, 1995), pp. 19–21.

215 "Takhsis arz va roshd 'mafiay varedat' dar Iran," [Allocation of Foreign Currency and Growth of 'Imports Mafia' in Iran] *Manoto TV*, April 10, 2012; and "Naboodi eshteghal ba varedat enhesartalabaneh," [Annihilation of Employment by Monopolized Imports] *Tejarat*, September 14, 2017, p. 3.

216 "Tahrimha miravand, chin nemiravad," [Sanctions will Go, China won't] *Ghanoon Daily*, April 8, 2015, p. 8; and "Bazar Iran dar ghabzeh brandhay khareji," [Iranian Market in the Clutches of Foreign Brands] *Tabnak*, July 31, 2015.

ily-gained advantages because of a change in government or relevant officials.[217] Moreover, an important factor behind the size and performance of
the mafia was the overall situation of Iranian economy and its varied interactions with the outside world.[218]

During the presidency of Ahmadinejad, a confluence of these effective factors tremendously empowered the imports mafia. The international regime
of stinging sanctions was only to inject fresh blood into the invidious tenta-
cles of the mafia in both internal and external realms of the Iranian economy.
When the crippling sanctions tightened their grapple upon the international
trade of Iran, the government sometimes found itself on the whims of the
mafia to muddle through. This situation was quite unambiguous since the
government had partially given some green light, either implicitly or explicitly, to the imports mafia to do something about circumventing the annoying
sanctions.[219] Moreover, part of the blocked oil money had to be returned back
in the form of commodities produced by a number of foreign countries. Obviously, not everybody from the private sector can be trusted with this daunting task, nor do all the public institutions themselves have enough capacity
and skills to single-handedly manage such a mega operation.[220]

In the domestic market, profit was the only factor behind the survival
and success of the imports mafia. The consumer market was huge and the
demand simply insatiable. Many people did not care whether the country
was under a savage regime of international sanctions; they were adamant to
buy whatever they wished to buy, regardless of who had produced it or how
those foreign goods had ended up in their markets and local stores.

---

217 "Tahrimha mafiay eghtesadi ra gostaresh dadeh ast," [Sanctions Have Expanded
the Economic Mafia] *Tabnak*, April 6, 2015; "Ba yek telephone jens arzan vared
mikonand!" [They Import Cheap Product with a Phone Call] *Tabnak*, June 20, 2016;
"Sadrat peste dar dast mafia," [Pistachio Exports in the Clutches of Mafia] *Jahan
Sanat*, October 17, 2017, pp. 1, 12.
218 "Enhesar bazar Iran dar dastan chashbadamiha, hojoom brandhay lavazem khanegi khareji be bazar Iran," [Iranian Markets Monopolized by Almond-eyes, Invasion
of Iranian Markets by Foreign Furniture Brands] *Khabar Eghtesadi*, May 15, 2013; and
"Anche varedat bar sar keshvar avard mogholha nayavardand," [Imports Harmed the
Country Worse than Mongols] *Jahan News*, July 5, 2015.
219 "How Iran Uses Dual Citizenship in the Caribbean to Skirt Sanctions," *The
National Interest*, December 23, 2014.
220 "Analysis: StanChart Hit May Not Dog Other Banks as Much as Feared," *Reuters*,
September 4, 2012; and "Credit Agricole to Pay $787 Million in Iran Sanctions
Accord," *Bloomberg*, October 20, 2015.

This situation was only exacerbated as more and more adults and young couples developed a taste for luxury and gave up their erstwhile lifestyle, succumbing to all the trappings of sumptuous goods and extravagant items shipped from a Western or Eastern country.[221] And the mafia was surely more than happy to import and deliver as early as possible various luxurious and expensive products (for some of which affluent customers were willing to pay more than double their original price in the source country).[222] But were Korean companies clueless about such delightful distributors of their products in Iran?

Part of the imports mafia was actually official or unofficial representative of different Korean companies inside Iran. They had been given certain privileges and rather exclusive rights to import a number of Korean brands. Koreans themselves had developed relatively good relationship with the people who played key roles in managing such affairs. They were to be regularly invited to various workshops and exhibitions regularly or occasionally convened somewhere in the ROK. Visa restrictions and bureaucratic red tape were kept to a minimum in order to facilitate better connections and close cooperation between both parties.[223] If special circumstances required, things could be simply managed indirectly and through a third party. That is why the diplomatic missions of the ROK or the primary representatives of the East Asian country's companies were often waiting in their wings to assist in any possible manner the role of various intermediaries to smooth the way for the shipment of more Korean commodities into Iran.[224]

---

221 "Iran's Love of Cars Survives Devastating Sanctions," *The National*, April 23, 2014; "Iranian Car Imports Rise by 150% after Easing of Sanctions," *The National*, September 13, 2014; "18 milyard dollar kharj safarhay khareji Iranian," [Foreign Travels of Iranians Cost $18 Billion] *Tabnak*, August 13, 2015; and "Iran goorestan mashinalat dar khavarmyaneh," [Iran the Graveyard of Machinery in the Middle East] *Tabnak*, November 25, 2015.

222 "Lavazem khanegi Irani ghorbani mafiay varedkonandeh," [Iranian Furniture a Casualty of Imports Mafia] *Jahan-e Sanat*, June 19, 2016, p. 12; and "Dolat eshteghalzae kard amma baray kharejiha!" [Government Created Jobs but for Foreigners!] *Kayhan*, October 9, 2016, pp. 1, 2.

223 "Bazar Iran behesht koreiha dar sal toolid melli!" [Iranian Market the Paradise of Koreans in the Year of National Production!] *Asr Iran*, October 8, 2012; "Ijad shoghl baray korye jenoobi va chin: Bohran bikari dar Iran," [Job Creation for South Korea and China: The Crisis of Unemployment in Iran] *Rooz Online*, November 28, 2013; and "Jozeyat jaded az varedat khodroo ba arz daroo," [New Details about Importing Cars by Drugs' Foreign Exchange] *Tabnak*, October 13, 2015.

224 "Ship and Air Links to Iran Are Slowly Being Reknit," *Korea Joongang Daily*, March 10, 2016.

The Role of Smuggling and the Black Market

As a corollary to the international sanctions and other barriers to normal business and free trade, smuggling and off the books economy widely flourished in Iran from one year to another. Importing goods and foreign currency into the country became extremely difficult, but selling products to other countries or transferring cash to other destinations, even for strictly educational expenses, was not really an easy business either.[225] This pesky problem had already existed in the country in various forms, but the new regime of crippling sanctions aggravated the situation unprecedentedly. The private sector and ordinary citizens were burdened with a welter of annoying impediments and obstacles to their usual business activities, and government institutions and even foreign stakeholders were ineluctably affected in one way or another. As a case in point, the South Korean ambassador to Iran once revealed that his embassy had to smuggle its funds into Iran because of the international sanctions targeting financial transactions with Tehran.[226]

Meanwhile, unemployment chronically exacerbated the state of smuggling and black market dealings. Of course, the sanctions themselves had corrosive implications for job creation and employment, but various dreadful restrictions and limitations stemming from those international measures were not the only culprit.[227] In addition to negative ramifications of the war and all ideological and political infightings, successive governments had not invested sufficiently to create enough opportunities for the growing number of young people entering the job markets. The system of higher education was also quickly producing more graduates who could not easily find a position pertinent to their educational background and skills. Under such lamentable conditions, a growing number of people naturally found that smuggling and participating in the off-the-books economy would be the best way to make ends meet, if not to make a fortune.[228]

---

225 "Iran, South Korea to Begin Economic Trade in Euro," *The Daily Star* (Lebanon), August 27, 2016.

226 "Safir kore: Pool sefarat ra ba ghachagh be Iran miavarim," [Korean Ambassador: We Smuggle Embassy Funds into Iran] *Tabnak*, July 11, 2016.

227 "S. Korean Bank Reprimanded for Illegal Money Transactions Involving Iranian Account," *Global Post*, May 7, 2014; and "Sanctions Eased, Iran Sends Black Market a Strategic Warning," *New York Times*, March 19, 2016.

228 "25 milyard dollar kalay ghachagh tavassot maraje rasmi!" [$25 Billion Smuggling Commodity through Formal Channels!] *Tabnak*, June 28, 2015; "27.6 darsad eghtesad

As far as Korean products were concerned, a major problem was the unlicensed importation of commodities from illegal venues. Regardless of its direct or indirect connections to a similar phenomenon of "suitcase trade trafficking," however, this form of bringing in Korean or other foreign goods had a lot to do with Iran's own borders. Extensive and porous borders had made it relatively easy to smuggle goods in from the neighboring countries, either directly or through intermediaries.[229] Moreover, a number of the free trade zones, mostly located close to the borders, contributed to this gray-market.[230] Many people living close to those borders had plenty of motivation to buy foreign goods at cheaper prices and then sell them to their fellow citizens at a mark-up. The practice was not always fail-proof, and sometimes people risked their capital and even their lives in order to make more money.[231]

Smuggling and the black market, plus suitcase trade trafficking, grew over time to an "industry" worth more than $10 billion, though it is often hard to estimate the real value of this type of commercial activities.[232] All of this also played an important role in furthering the ubiquitous presence of foreign products, including Korean brands, in the Iranian markets. The government often assigned a specific quota for the importation of certain foreign goods, but there was little to be done with the surfeit of products coming in through illegal channels. Neither it was really plausible to confiscate such items from local markets, nor did the government have any legal means to interfere with personal taste and shopping preferences of the citizenry.[233] At the end of the day, it was the government again which had to bear the

Iran gheirrasmi ast," [27.6 Percent of Iranian Economy is Informal] *Tabnak*, November 8, 2015; and "Varedat badkheim," [Ill-fated Imports] *Jamejam*, August 3, 2016, p. 1.

229 "Ijad eshteghal baray kharejiha ashk temsah baray kulbarha," [Job Creation for Foreigners Crocodile Tears for Porters] *Kayhan*, February 2, 2017, pp. 1, 4.

230 "Cheragh sabz parleman be darvazehay varedat kala," [Parliament's Green Light to the Gateways of Commodity Imports] *Shahr Ara*, August 25, 2016, p. 4.

231 "Killing of Porters and Arrests Persist in Kurdistan Border Regions," *Radio Zamaneh*, July 13, 2016; "70 darsad ghachagh kala rasmi miayad," [70 Percent of Commodity Smuggling Come Formal] *Hamshahri*, October 4, 2016, p. 4; and "70 darsad kalay ghachagh az mabadi ghanooni vared mishavad," [70 Percent of Smuggling Commodity Enter through Legal Channels] *Tejarat*, October 23, 2016, p. 5.

232 "Smugglers in Iran Make $20B a Year," *Trend News Agency*, November 27, 2015; and "Midanid 20 milyard dollar ghachagh che vazni darad?" [Do You Know the Load of $20 Billion Smuggling?] *Shahr Ara*, October 2, 2016.

233 "Iraniha be andazeh kol afrigha khodroo kharidand," [Car Purchase by Iranians on a Par with Entire African Continent] *Tabnak*, September 11, 2015.

brunt of criticisms and malicious censures from every side for neglecting the welfare and prosperity of the citizens by its policy of uncalculated imports — even when a segment of the citizenry had corrosively contributed to the malaise.[234]

But the government had to do something about it, because the problem had taken a great toll and hastened the erosion of domestic production and national brands, which exacerbated the current dismal conditions of unemployment and job creation in the country.

More recently, new laws and regulations have been enacted, while a widespread approach of tightening monitoring mechanisms and security checks has aimed to systematically fight the practice. In spite of such measures, nonetheless, it is unlikely the government will succeed to eliminate the problem in total any time soon. Even if everything was put into good order domestically sometime in near future, little can be actually done with regard to the ongoing situation in a number of the neighboring counties which have long been a source of smuggled commodities into the Iranian markets.[235] In an ideal situation, however, such circumstances may just get reversed so that Iran itself becomes a source of trafficked foreign goods into those countries because it shares long and porous borders with them.

A Less Visible Factor: From Being a Model To Being the Contrary

The foregoing parameters all certainly played a part in the pervasive presence of Korean products in Iran, but there were still other components which inconspicuously turned out to be instrumental in Korea's successful market penetration. In particular, the way that the ROK was introduced in Iran over the years made the environment conducive to its achievements there. As a sharp contrast to the Koreans' approach to Iran during the past decades, their country received, by and large, positive coverage in academic

---

234 "Zanjir ghachagh bar pay eghtesad moghavemati," [Chain of Smuggling at the Foot of Resistance Economy] *Jamejam*, June 20, 2016, p. 4; and "Ghachagh, salyaneh 20 hezar forsat shoghli va nabood mikonad," [Smuggling Destroys 20,000 Jobs Annually] *Shahrvand Daily*, August 17, 2016, pp. 1, 4.

235 "Turkey, South Korea Sign Major Trade Deal," *Hurriyet Daily News*, June 9, 2014; "Toolid melli faday varedat!" [National Production Sacrificed for Imports!] *Jahan News*, February 2, 2015; "Turkey -- Brother Nation of Korea," *Korea Times*, November 15, 2015; and "Labi ghavi ghachaghchian," [The Powerful Lobby of Smugglers] *Jahan-e Sanat*, July 25, 2016, pp. 1, 12.

and policy circles as well as in various media outlets.[236] Even in the midst of a temporary fuss over a given economic issue or a fleeting disturbance over a political matter, South Korea emerged victoriously, overall. Minor disruptions did not stop the forward momentum.

Why and how did the Korean trajectory turn out to be so much more successful than the somber fate of Iran? In countless academic meetings and other professional gatherings, for instance, many speakers used to make a comparison between the Iranian and Korean automobile industries, as they were begun roughly at a same period of time. Other pundits and specialists proffered different data and statistics to substantiate their views with regard to comparative economic arguments or assumptions. Another class of rather erudite academics and balanced experts tended to recall various contentious issues from a period when Iranians themselves were actually a role model for Koreans, no matter that their paths of development soon diverged.

As a rump of a small, divided country, when the ROK embarked on its industrialization and development programs in the early 1960s, it was far behind Iran and most other countries in terms of almost all important economic and social characteristics. Their historical backgrounds were not at all comparable, either. Even Korean car makers that had launched their factories at the same time, they typically needed to dispatch representatives to consult with their Iranian counterparts to inquire about their achievements and progress.

A similar story was common in the education sector, where some high profile academics from the ROK might promote the Iranian record as a model worth emulating.[237] There were various areas ranging from the aviation industry to the health system which had once captured the attention of various Korean officials and experts as an Iranian success story, even if the narrative would be evaluated differently by later generations in each country.

All such views and arguments have been around on and off for the past several decades, and their popularity has helped to build South Korea's image in a way that is conducive to the success of its products in Iran. As some ideological proclivities and political passions within the larger Iranian soci-

---

236 "S. Korean Envoy Cuts Ribbon on Handicraft Exhibit in Tehran," *Tehran Times*, October 24, 2016.
237 "Investment in Education Spurs Nat'l Development," *Korea Times*, January 30, 1977, p. 5.

ety have gradually abated in favor of material matters and economic forces in more recent years, more fresh attention has been shifted toward success stories of other nations. Commentators across the political spectrum have pointed to the Korean story as something at least worth learning from.[238] They have been particularly enthusiastic when special occasions provided them with a unique chance to get their message across.[239] During Park's visit to Iran in May 2016, for instance, a flurry of commentaries and media reports recycled these debates, giving prominence to some economic statistics and social data about the ROK.[240]

This tendency has ineluctably instilled in the minds of many Iranian citizens the impression that the Korean story has been rather spectacular, such that many of them now praise their own taste for buying Korean brands in larger quantity. It also unintentionally provided officials in the public sector and merchants in the private domain with justifications to import even a greater share of Korean products one year after another.

But Iran is finally coming in from the cold, and the development mantra is increasingly becoming a universal discussion within the society itself. Does the Korean story provide a good guideline to learn from? Is it really an appropriate blueprint for societies like Iran in the first place?

In Search of a Model: From a Second Secular Japan
    to an Islamic Korea in the Making

Modernization and progress have been riveting themes within Iranian society since the 19th century. Such discussions were first constrained to the intellectual and policy circles of the capital and other major cities. With the ascendancy of the Pahlavi dynasty in the early decades of the 20th century, however, development and modernization practically became the mandate of the state.

From that point on, the main approach to and the ways of transforming the traditional Iranian society became hotly contested issues in all academ-

238 "Speaker: S. Korea's Experience Can Help Iran's Economic Growth," *Fars News Agency,* June 22, 2014.
239 "FM: Seoul Attaches Special Importance to Ties with Tehran," *Fars News Agency,* April 23, 2014; and "Iran Experts Views," *Arirang News,* November 6, 2015.
240 "Cheragh sabz bazar Iran be khodroohay korei!" [Iran Market's Greenlight to Korean Cars!] *Tabnak,* June 7, 2011; and "Chera Iran Koreye jenoobi nemishavad?" [Why Doesn't Iran Become South Korea?] *Setareh Sobh,* May 23, 2016, pp. 1, 7.

ic meetings, policy circles, and social gatherings. There was no consensus among the literati as to the most desirable model or the goal of the modernization process. The state was not rudderless, but it had not managed to mobilize a clear majority of the country's elites behind its quest for transformation and progress. Many people simply could not succumb to a Western-style approach toward modernization, although that model had many ardent proponents in both academic and policy circles.

For these people, Iran has had its own distinctive identity and ought not to sacrifice its unique characteristics just for the sake of becoming a modern state. Moreover, they were largely against swift socio-economic changes which had potential to wreak havoc on the country's cultural values and moral moorings. Their insistence on retaining the native attributes and customs of the country put the state in a rather defensive position. The government and its stalwarts behind the modernization programs had to justify their intentions, denying that they were forfeiting their own national customs and characteristics by replacing them with values and norms imported from the West. The idea of making a "second Japan" was aimed in part to give the impression that the country was going to preserve its own national identity while moving fast to achieve milestones in the economic and technological areas. The Pahlavi dynasty, however, soon collapsed and the country failed to emerge as a new Japan in the Middle East.[241]

With the ascendancy of the Islamic Republic, intense discussions about modernization and development subsided somewhat, but they never disappeared from the public discourse. After an initial period of trial and error, the objective was to accomplish a certain degree of economic and technological progress without forsaking the country's identity and cultural values. That is why some people raised the idea of creating an "Islamic Japan" according to which Iran could preserve its peculiar religious characteristics while proceeding to structurally transform its economic and technological attributes.

What both the ideas of a "second secular Japan" and "Islamic Japan" had in common was that Iran did not wish to become a Westernized society by being alienated from its historical mission and national traditions. As more

---

241 William Shawcross, *The Shah's Last Ride: The Story of the Exile, Misadventures and Death of the Emperor* (New York: Touchstone, 1989), p. 174.

time elapsed, however, the catchy yet shallow notion of "Islamic Japan" turned out to be unfeasible and was consigned to the historical archives.

In more recent years, development and progress have once again become a leitmotiv of various academic think tanks and policy circles in Iran. Dismayed with or disappointed in foreign models and imported frameworks, some people have even become creative in carving out new ideas for economic and social transformation. For instance, they passionately lecture about an "innovative" version of development dubbed the "Islamic-Iranian model" or "Iranian-Islamic model," without providing convincing details about the practical steps to implement their visionary blueprint. Moreover, this new generation of "nativists" does not seem to have much sway over what is done in practice by the government and public institutions. One might predict that the end result will neither satisfy the champions of imported models nor fulfill the dreams of those who fervently favor an indigenous pattern of progress for the country.

A major stumbling block to the realization of either approach is that Iran has already missed lots of opportunities to achieve something remarkable,[242] and the current generation is in no mood to continue sacrificing for the general good. The society is increasingly moving toward a crass materialistic realm where personal interests prevent people from sacrificing their own immediate welfare for the sake of their country. The birth rate is falling fast, the society is aging, and the class gap is deepening unprecedentedly. These tragic trends are also highly visible in Europe and throughout East Asia, but the trend has accelerated in the ROK and in Iran perhaps faster than anywhere else.[243]

---

242 "Iran Has Potential to Extract Up to 80 Minerals: Official," *Trend News Agency*, January 7, 2014; "250 Million People Feast on Iran Horticulture," *Press TV*, September 24, 2015; "Iran 5th Engineer Trainer in World: VP," *Mehr News Agency*, October 14, 2015; "Iran's Priciest Export Isn't Oil, It's Caviar," *New York Post*, November 13, 2015; and "Iran's 'Black Gold' Exports Thrive," *Press TV*, December 7, 2015.
243 "300 nafar 60 darsad pool keshavr ra darand" [300 People Own 60 Percent of the Country's Money], *Tabnak*, December 14, 2012; "Iran's Identity Crisis," *Foreign Policy*, October 5, 2015; "Corruption among Iran's Business Elites," *Deutsche Welle*, March 14, 2016; "Fury Erupts in Iran over Vast Salaries Paid to Government Officials," *Guardian*, June 17, 2016; and "Iran to Cap Government Pay," *Bloomberg*, July 27, 2016.

Table 1. Fertility rate (births/woman) in Iran, Japan, and South Korea, selected years

Country	1960	1979	1988	2016
Iran	6.93	6.4	5.5	1.7
Japan	2.00	1.8	1.7	1.4
South Korea	6.09	2.9	1.6	1.2

Source: *The World Bank*

Iran did not catch up with its counterparts from East Asia based on their developmental plans, but it has a huge potential to surpass them in terms of their present characteristics. At the end of the day, therefore, it looks likely that Iran is increasingly moving toward the creation of an "Islamic Korea," and that is why many in South Korea are really eager to forge even deeper connections to this speedily changing Persian Gulf country.

Vowing to Follow a New Course: Turning Trade
Ties Into Strategic Economic Relations

Besides its critical political significance, Park Geun-hye's visit to Tehran had pivotal economic implications for Korea's commercial interactions with Iran. Accompanied by "the largest business delegation in the history of Korean presidential trips," her economic mission to Iran was to eventually benefit all those 236 participating entities, involving representatives of 146 small and medium-sized companies, 38 giant corporations, and 52 bodies affiliated with business organizations, public institutions, and hospitals.

Park particularly upped the ante when she dubbed Iran "a land of opportunity" and urged her fellow citizens on multiple occasions to create a "second Middle East boom" by taking advantage of the huge opportunities Iran could present.[244] In addition to its present status as the holder of the largest reserves of natural gas and the fourth-largest oil deposits in the world, a new rising Iran could offer lots of other possibilities to make the dream of Koreans for a second boom in the region come true.[245]

---

244 "Korean Companies to Build Hospitals in Iran," *Business Korea*, June 5, 2015; "Iran is Land of Opportunity: Park," *Korea Times*, May 4, 2016; "Enhanced Ties with Iran to Boost Exports, Job Creation: Report," *Yonhap News Agency*, May 11, 2016; and "2nd Middle East Boom Expected: S. Korea Made Agreement for Largest-ever Economic Cooperation with Iran," *Business Korea*, July 4, 2016.

245 "Park Seeks to Generate 'Second Middle East Boom'," *Korea Herald*, March 2, 2015; "Second Middle East Boom," *Korea Herald*, March 3, 2015; "President Park Asks Country's Leaders to Help Boost Ties with Middle East," *Arirang News*, March 13, 2015; "Park Calls for 2nd Middle East Boom," *Korea Times*, March 19, 2015; "Iran, South Korea

During Park's visit to Iran, a flurry of lucrative deals were signed between the two countries, including 66 MOUs, most of which had to do with bilateral economic interactions. It was estimated that such agreements were worth more than $37 billion, providing a better ground for various Korean companies to participate in many new projects in Iran ranging from construction to energy facilities.

In a press conference after their summit, Rouhani and Park also promised to rev up their economic relationship from about $6 billion to more than $18 billion in the future, though such a figure sounded less impressive given the fact that Rouhani and the Chinese president Xi Jinping had just vowed to increase the volume of their countries' economic relations to some $600 billion during the latter's official visit to Iran in early 2016.[246] Moreover, the East Asian country announced that its president had decided to spike her "biggest-ever economic accomplishment" with generosity by unveiling a $25 billion finance package, apparently the largest of such kind, in order to help its companies to better take part in a number of joint projects in the Persian Gulf country.[247]

Meanwhile, Rouhani urged Park to work together with Iran for "turning trade relations to deep-rooted and strategic economic relations." There was certainly much hidden in this new official dialogue between the two sides, as Iran was already obsessed with how to transform its bilateral interactions with foreign countries from a zero-sum relationship into a win-win partnership.[248]

South Korea was one of those countries which was a target of Iran's new politico-economic approach toward the outside world. This is probably one reason why the stated figure for the prospective commercial connections between Tehran and Seoul was to be only some 3 percent of the volume proposed by Tehran and Beijing. Iran did not wish to permanently maintain its

---

to Launch Shipbuilding JV," *Press TV*, December 5, 2015; "Park's Approval Rating up after Trip to Iran," *Yonhap News Agency*, May 9, 2016; and "Daewoo Shipbuilding to Manage Iranian Shipbuilder," *Korea Times*, May 16, 2016.

246 "Iran, China Agree $600 billion Trade Deal after Sanctions," *Reuters*, January 23, 2016; and "Iran and South Korea Set to Triple Trade to $18 bn," *AFP*, May 2, 2016.

247 "Korea–Iran Summit Paves Way for $45.6b Business Deals," *Korea Herald*, May 2, 2016.

248 "Iran, South Korea Must Boost Strategic Ties: Rouhani," *Press TV*, May 2, 2016; and "Seoul, Tehran Expand Decades-long Friendship to Economic Partnership," *Yonhap News Agency*, May 10, 2016.

present format and pace of economic relations with South Korea. Nor had Iran really hoped that the ROK's overall approach to business with Iran was to undergo seismic changes any time soon.

The bottom line was that Koreans needed to bring in hard capital and particularly technology if they wished to develop stronger commercial connections to the country and thereby preserve their share in the Iranian markets.[249] They could no longer take the Persian Gulf country's trade opportunities for granted; other competitors were waiting in the wings to snap them up.[250] In fact, the relationship — which some officials of the two countries had sometimes considered to be "complementary" — could not last much longer.

While it was ultimately possible for Iran to replace Korean products with similar items from other countries such as China, the ROK was not in a position to easily find a market as large and lucrative as the one presented by the Iranians.[251] Of course, Iran had to for now supply some of its energy resources to the ROK in order to considerably empower its enervated financial muscles, but even this aspect of Iran's external interactions could undergo significant changes soon or later.[252]

After all, Koreans were not the only foreigners who heard new demands from Tehran; Iran had already presented some or all of such preconditions to a range of other high-profile politico-economic delegates which had visited the country since the early presidency of Hassan Rouhani.[253] That is why

249 "Korean Firms Invited to Invest in Iran," *Tasnim News Agency*, October 29, 2014; "Yun Byungse: Koreans Impatiently Waiting to Enter Iranian Market," *Tehran Times*, November 8, 2015; "S. Korean Firm Exports Electronic ID Cards to Iran," *Yonhap News Agency*, July 7, 2016; and "Iran–South Korea Technology Exchange Center Inaugurated," *Tehran Times*, August 29, 2016.

250 "Ultimatum Iran be koreiha: Toolid ra moshtarek nakonid, tarefeh dobarabar mishavad," [Iran Ultimatum to Koreans: If not Engage in Joint Production, Tariffs Double] *Asr Iran*, July 20, 2015.

251 "'Remorseful' South Korea Returns to Iran," *Press TV*, August 24, 2015; "Deputy FM to Visit Iran for Policy Talks," *Yonhap News Agency*, September 7, 2015; "Major Leap in S. Korea's Imports of Iran Oil," *Tasnim News Agency*, May 16, 2016; "Doosan Heavy Signs $185m Plant Deal in Iran," *Korea Joongang Daily*, June 28, 2016; and "Business Deals From Iran: H & Surgical Signs $2 Million Contract during Iran Trip," *Business Korea*, June 30, 2016.

252 "Korea Faces Hurdles to Do Business with Iran," *Korea Times*, February 10, 2014; and "Iran Refused to Let Park's Plane Fly Over," *Chosun Ilbo*, June 3, 2014.

253 "Ehday 4 khodroo az souy koreye jenoobi be doolat Iran," [South Korea Presented 4 Automobiles to Iranian Government] *Asr Iran*, February 14, 2016; "Enhesar zodaei az varedat khodroo," [Breaking the Monopoly of Car Imports] *Taadol*, June 21, 2016, p. 12; "Sarmayehgozari shart varedat khodroo," [Investment a Requisite for Car

a large number of those sanguine and hopeful delegations immediately returned home crestfallen and empty-handed.

Iran wanted a new economic and financial partnership which could soon translate into domestic production and job creation, but most of those delegates were arriving from countries that were themselves suffering from distressing economic depression and high levels of unemployment.[254] In a nutshell, they were largely interested in selling their products and services to Iran in exchange for ready cash.[255]

The economic situation in South Korea was not as bleak as some of those countries, but was the East Asian state up to doing business in Iran anyway?

Limits to Capital and Technology Transfer

There are a number of impediments facing any significant financial and technological shipment from the ROK to Iran. First, the Koreans themselves did not easily get the capital and technology they needed when they commenced the country's successive phases of industrialization and development. At each juncture, they had to jump through hoops to achieve anything close to what they initially desired. In some cases, they even had to submit to further national humiliation for the sake of accumulating enough capital and financial resources to implement their development programs. And to get access to advanced machinery and technology, their mission was often tougher; Koreans were sometimes required to offer certain crucial privileges and rights to foreign stakeholders in exchange for what they needed. Hard-nosed people normally emerge from tough circumstances, so it seems unlikely that Koreans would really be willing to give away on a silver platter what they themselves had attained only after working their fingers to the bone.

Second, in spite of its breathtaking industrial and technological achievements over the past several decades, South Korea is, as always, dependent on the whims of some other nations for the next generation of updated systems

Imports] *Hamshahri*, December 3, 2016, p. 4; and "Iran's Investment Pledge for Korean Biotech City Makes No Progress," *Yonhap News Agency*, September 7, 2016.

254 "Reghabat bayad baray enteghal technology be Iran bashad; zhapon va koreye jenoobi gozinehay sharghi va moghabel brandhay gharbi," [Rivalry Should be over Technology Transfer to Iran; Japan and South Korea Eastern Options vs. Western Brands] *Iranian Labour News Agency (ILNA)*, July 31, 2015.

255 "'Iran to Sign Preferential Trade Agreements with 5 More Countries'," *Tehran Times*, July 7, 2014; and "Foreign Automakers Find Iranian Market Has Gone Local," *Korea Herald*, December 1, 2014.

and technical know-how for its high-tech juggernaut. The United States and Japan in particular play a pivotal role in replenishing such critical requirements for South Korea in one way to another. As a case in point, a great deal of the ROK's trade deficit with Japan is attributed to the former's regular importation of technology and advanced equipment from Tokyo. This matter is still different than some other often stealthy and surreptitious moves taken by a number of high profile Korean companies seeking to maintain their present international reputation and competitive edge.[256] It is, therefore, unrealistic to expect that Korean companies would be inclined to quickly pass on to other countries their hard-gained latest techniques.[257]

Third, the issue of cost and affordability can determine the scope of cooperation between Korean companies and their foreign partners. A number of major Korean corporations such as Kia and Hyundai have long engaged in joint projects in different parts of Iran, while other companies like Samsung and LG have more recently demonstrated willingness to share some of their technology with Iranians by working on a number of fairly profitable projects.[258] Things may work well for both sides, at least for a while, but others are aggressively joining the race.[259] The Europeans, Germans in particular, want to win back their previous market shares, while some ravenous Chinese companies such as Huawei have promised to break Samsung's mobile

---

256 "Jury Awards $1 Billion to Apple in Samsung Patent Case," *New York Times*, August 24, 2012; "Samsung to Pay Ericsson $650 Million Plus Royalties to End Patent Spat," *Reuters*, January 27, 2014; "Apple, Samsung Call Patent Truce Outside U.S.," *Wall Street Journal*, August 5, 2014; "Hyundai Loses $28.9 Million Patent Trial over Hybrid Engines," *Bloomberg*, October 2, 2015; "LG Ordered to Cough Up $3.5 Million in Patent Violations," *Digital Trends*, March 27, 2016; "US Court Shields Korean CD-ROM Manufacturer in Patent Fight," *Wall Street Journal*, July 6, 2016; and "Samsung Chief Lee Arrested as South Korean Corruption Probe Deepens," *Reuters*, February 17, 2017.

257 Howard Pack, "Asian Successes VS. Middle Eastern Failures: The Role of Technology Transfer in Economic Development," *Issues in Science and Technology*, Vol. XXIV, No, 3 (Spring 2008), pp. 47–54.

258 "Modiramel Samsung dar Iran dar pasokh be Farf: Elam amadegi baray toolid mobile va tablet dar Iran," [Samsung CEO in Iran in Reply to Fars: Ready to Produce Mobile and Tablet in Iran] *Fars News Agency*, December 30, 2014; and "Iran–South Korea Technology Exchange Center Inaugurated," *Tehran Times*, August 30, 2016, pp. 1, 4.

259 "Minister Says More Mideast Reactors Planned," *Korea Joongang Daily*, May 28, 2014; "Developing Countries Explore Ways to Boost Korea Ties," *Korea Herald*, October 22, 2014; "Hyundai to Invest in Iran's Anzali Port," *Press TV*, August 18, 2015; and "Iran's IDRO, South Korea's Hyundai Sign Cooperation Document," *Tasnim News Agency*, August 7, 2016.

monopoly in Iran.[260] Iranians may refuse to import some Korean industrial equipment and technical know-how because of their relatively high costs, and current or prospective joint ventures will probably encounter serious, if not fatal, competition from a slew of Western and Eastern contenders.[261]

Fourth, technical and legal frameworks have represented obstacles for foreign investors in their host countries. In exchange for bringing in their capital and technology, Korean companies may demand from Iran certain rights and privileges which the Iranian government is unable to grant because of laws and regulations. The Iranian constitution is straightforward in terms of the maximum sway a foreign stakeholder can hold while negotiating a deal with the government.[262] Although various laws and legal codes have been either revised or freshly enacted by the country in recent years to pave the way for more foreign investment and technological imports into Iran, the country still remains rather conservative compared to some others in the region.[263] In a joint venture, actual authority and even management style may be areas of contention when two parties have contrasting cultural mores and work ethics. All this will ultimately influence the health and longevity of their shared projects.[264]

---

260 "110-member Chinese Trade Delegation to Visit Iran Next Week," *Tehran Times*, February 22, 2014; "China Reaps Rewards for Standing by Iran, *The Hindu*, April 11, 2015; "Doornamay ravabet shir qorran va ezhdhay khizan," [Prospect of Relations between Roaring Lion and Rising Dragon] *Khabar Online*, July 28, 2015; and "S. Korean Goods' Presence in Iran Falls amid Rise of China," *Yonhap News Agency*, January 23, 2016.

261 "East Asian Lessons for the Middle East," *Gulf Times*, April 3, 2011; "President: S. Korean Companies Willing to Partner in Iran's Projects," *Fars News Agency*, August 9, 2014; "I See Bright Future for Tehran–Seoul Relations: Korean Minister," *Tehran Times*, September 20, 2015; and "Iran–South Korea Joint Economic Committee Meeting Due in Feb.," *Tehran Times*, January 23, 2016.

262 "Shart Hyundai baray montazh khodroo dar Iran," [Hyundai Proviso for Car Assembly in Iran] *Donya-e Eqtesad*, September 12, 2015.

263 "Iran, South Korea to Discuss Post-sanctions Cooperation in Seoul," *Press TV*, June 10, 2015; "Iran Urges Koreans to Invest in Oil Plans," *Press TV*, September 15, 2015; "Iranian Officials to Learn Environment Technology in S Korea," *Mehr News Agency*, July 15, 2016; and "Iran, Korea Sign Oil Deal," *Mehr News Agency*, July 19, 2016.

264 "Iranian, S. Korean Officials Discuss Cooperation in Mining Sector," *Fars News Agency*, April 23, 2014; "Iran Hoping for Korean Companies' Participation in Infrastructure Projects," *Business Korea*, January 12, 2015; "Iran to Use South Korean Technology in 4G Mobile Internet Project," *Trend News Agency*, January 13, 2015; "Iran, South Korea to Cooperate on Steel Production," *Fars News Agency*, February 1, 2015; "S. Korea, Iran to Boost IT, Science Cooperation," *Korea Times*, May 2, 2016; and "Iranian, S. Korean Companies Ink Two MOUs on Coop in South Pars Gas Field," *Tehran Times*, May 25, 2016.

Last but not least is the role of political will and strategic considerations involving one or more other stakeholders. The possibility is high that South Korea will eventually reach a limit and will not go beyond a certain point in sharing with Iran its crucial technical attainments — supposing that the East Asian country is really willing to share them in the first place.

A great deal of this will, of course, depend on the ultimate shape and pattern of Iran's overall relationship with the West, and particularly the United States.[265] If Iran continues to maintain its current status in the rival camp within the present pecking order of the international system, the ROK will assuredly be dependent on the whims of the Americans for any closer politico-economic ties as well as technological connections to Tehran. And if, improbably, things moved in the reverse direction, the political will in Seoul would determine the size and scope of joint projects with Iran.[266]

Table 2. International ranking based on nominal gross domestic product (GDP) 2016

Country	GDP (US$MM)	Rank
South Korea	1,411,245	11
Iran	425,402	25
North Korea	17,396	113

Source: *United Nations Statistics Division* available at unstats.un.org

Prospects for Iranian–North Korean Economic Ties

In sharp contrast to the ubiquitous presence of South Korean brands throughout Iran, it is almost impossible to find any trace of a North Korean product or commodity in that country. It seems that the reclusive communist state of the DPRK has practically never had any physical, material presence in Iran, while various stories about close connections between the two parties run from myth to fairy tale. Of course, North Korea has long maintained a functioning embassy in Tehran, and its diplomatic envoys regularly travel to different parts of Iran. People from North Korea (no matter who

---

265 Geoffrey Kemp, "U.S.–Iranian Strategic Cooperation since 1979," in Henry Sokolski and Patrick Clawson, eds., *Checking Iran's Nuclear Ambitions* (Washington, DC: Strategic Studies Institute, 2004), pp. 101–112; and Wright, pp. 189–191.
266"Bazdid sarzadeh Jahangiri az Samsung," [Jahangiri's Surprise Visit to Samsung] *Rah Mardom Daily*, June 2, 2016, p. 1; "Dollar az mobadlat Iran va koreye jenoobi hazf shod," [Dollar Eliminated from Iran and South Korea Exchanges] *Tabnak*, August 26, 2016; and "Chegooneh koreye jenoobi sevvomin sharik tejari Iran shod?" [How Did South Korea Become Iran's Third Trading Partner?] *Tabnak*, September 12, 2017.

they are) also enjoy rights and freedoms in Iran similar to other foreigners, whether they visit the country temporarily or live there for some time. But it is still hard for an average Iranian citizen inside the country to meet someone from North Korea in person, while a flurry of South Korean nationals, be they diplomats and company officials or tourists and university students, are easy to recognize in Tehran and some other major cities.[267]

Moreover, North Korea is absent from data and statistics released regularly by the government agencies and public institutions in Iran. When an annual report on foreign trade is issued, it is often hard to find any direct reference to the DPRK, which gives the impression that there was no commercial activity involving the two parties worth mentioning. Some official reports and accounts on Iran's commercial relationship with the outside world simply drop North Korea from the text, while in some other works the records for the communist East Asian state might be incorporated into different categories such as "trade with other countries," "unreported," "undeclared," "unknown," etc.

For some time, the interactions between Iran and the DPRK touched upon sensitive matters which required special attention. It was often a matter of national security not to divulge data related to certain aspects of bilateral cooperation between Tehran and Pyongyang. Sometimes this was done intentionally, to stave off any abuse and interference by other countries that keep an eye on any sort of official and unofficial interactions between the two countries. In other, less pressing circumstances, the approach could be just an innocuous tactic to keep certain things quiet in order to mislead rivals and keep them guessing.

But the situation has hardly been much different in the international press. Media outlets and policy periodicals regularly publish too much about military and political connections between North Korea and Iran, while hardly bothering to find out what, if anything, was going on between the two sides economically.[268] Their data and statistics, assuming they were all plausible and meticulously reported, overwhelmingly focused on aspects

---

267 "A North Korean in Iran," *Foreign Policy*, July 23, 2014.
268 "Iran, North Korea Sign Technology Agreement," *Huffington Post*, September 1, 2012; "Iran, North Korea to Discuss Development of Bilateral Relations," *Trend News Agency*, February 23, 2014; and "Iran, N Korea Eye Coop. in Tobacco Industry," *Mehr News Agency*, September 20, 2015.

of missiles and conventional military cooperation between the DPRK and Iran.[269] Even the South Korean think tanks and security institutions, which have long kept a beady eye on almost every single aspect of Pyongyang's connections to the outside world, often failed to report much about North Korean economic and financial relations with Iran. In fact, this less-noticed component of the DPRK–Iran relationship has long been buried under an avalanche of strategic objectives, politically-oriented information or disinformation, and expedient measures.

After all, when Iran needed to buy something from North Korea, it did not always have to pay ready cash. Nor was everything Tehran imported from Pyongyang essentially military in nature. The two countries, therefore, decided to sometimes engage in a system of barter so that Tehran could repay Pyongyang using some valuable commodity other than money.[270] Energy resources, oil in particular, were one such item which the DPRK desperately needed to survive, having lost its regular supply from the Soviet Union or China.[271]

Such a pattern of international trade between Iran and North Korea might also involve a third party, especially China, because Pyongyang did not always have enough sophisticated commercial vessels to handle its business with Tehran. Even when North Korea could manage its own non-military commercial interactions directly with Iran, the long distance between the two countries required another party to guard the sea lines for any Pyongyang-bound ship carrying oil or any other Iranian product.[272]

In the future, a big part of Iranian–North Korean economic ties, like their political relations, will depend on the political environment of the Korean Peninsula.[273] If the present political system in Pyongyang survives in the long

269 "Thais Say North Korea Arms Were Iran-Bound," *New York Times*, January 31, 2010; "'Iran–North Korea Cooperation May Sabotage Nuclear Deal'," *The Weekly Standard*, June 2, 2015; and "'38 North' Raises Suspicion on N. Korea–Iran Missile Cooperation," *KBS World*, September 24, 2016.

270 "Molaghat vozaray omour kharejeh Iran va koreye shomali," [Iranian and North Korean Foreign Ministers Meet] *Tabnak*, May 26, 2011; and "Tavafogh Iran va koreye shomali baray tahator kala," [Iran and North Korea Agreement for Commodity Barter] *Tabnak*, April 22, 2013.

271 "Cash-strapped N. Korea Seen Trading Weapons for Iran Oil," *World Tribune*, December 8, 2015.

272 "Movafeghat kore shomali ba kharid naft az Iran," [North Korean Agreement to Buy Oil from Iran] *Tabnak*, April 23, 2013.

273 "With Iran Visit, South Korea Seeks Closer Ties to Pyongyang Ally," *Wall Street Journal*, April 28, 2016; and "Iran Complies with Resolution on N. Korea: Ambassador,"

run, it will certainly need to develop closer commercial connections to countries like Iran in order to implement its cautious projects of gradual economic development and political openness.

Iran may not need to keep up close military cooperation with North Korea any longer, and it may not be willing to continue conducting commercial interactions with the DPRK by barter, even when the business involves some degree of participation by a third party.[274] The growing role of the free market and money utilization in North Korea could partially make up for that, which would inject some new blood into the economic elements of Tehran–Pyongyang relations. After all, each country seems to be prudently preserving the other party as a valuable asset no matter what course of action their grand strategy will ultimately hinge upon.[275]

Korea Times, July 1, 2016.

274 "Iran Willing to Boost Ties with North Korea: VP," *Press TV*, October 9, 2013; "President Rouhani Calls for Expansion of Tehran–Pyongyang Ties," *Tasnim News Agency*, September 16, 2014; "Iran Working with North Korea to Thwart U.N. Nuclear Inspections: Report," *Washington Times*, September 4, 2015; and "U.S.–Iran Deal Could Lead to More Iranian Oil in N. Korea," *North Korea News*, December 7, 2015.

275 "Iran Committed to Maintaining Friendly Ties with North Korea," *Tasnim News Agency*, October 9, 2013; "President: Iran Supports Unity between North, South Korea," *Tasnim News Agency*, January 26, 2015; "N. Korea Seeking to Boost Trade with Iran: Envoy," *Tehran Times*, August 31, 2015; and "Pak daetongryeong 'Irangwa hanbando pihaeghwae daehan hyeoblyeog yeoji mandeuleo'," [President Park Talks of 'Cooperation with Iran on Denuclearization of the Korean Peninsula'] *Seoul Shinmun*, May 4, 2016.

Culture and Modern Economy

For ages, culture and the economy, as separate domains of human life, used to meet different longings and requirements of people around the world. In the contemporary era these two concepts surprisingly enough have connected up in various ways, but earlier, individuals as well as communities conventionally saw each of them as an autonomous sphere with relatively distinctive functions. And while culture certainly evolves and flows, it was in the area of economic circumstances where new developments gradually blurred the line between culture and economy. Later, additional industrial progress and technological advancement contributed to a growing interplay between culture and economy, so that they eventually ended up becoming entwined and hybridized. Some recent historical experiences particularly lend weight to the claims that today's highly economized cultures evolved as a result of exploiting cultural mores to serve specific economic objectives. As explained in detail by Max Weber in his magnum opus, *The Protestant Ethic and the Spirit of Capitalism*, certain cultural moorings and edifying values greatly helped a number of Western nations to swiftly overtake their equally resourceful counterparts in different parts of the world. Those successful countries subsequently took advantage of other cultural assets, including various Christian principles and symbols, to make inroads into new territories primarily for expanding their economic interests. When some other nations later emulated those stunning industrial and development stories, they had to similarly tap into other types of cultural resources in order to make headway toward achieving their newly-designed out national programs of modernization and progress. For instance the Japanese, who carefully evaluated the role of culture in both the edification and domination of Western nations, found it necessary to exaggerate and even fabricate certain cultural concepts in their history in order to galvanize the general public to work hard, in lock step, to achieve the national goals set since the beginning of the so-called Meiji restoration.[276]

As more and more nations embarked on similar industrialization and economic development plans throughout the world, the role of cultural elements also became more important, primarily in order to secure and then to solidify ever-increasing politico-economic interests among a growing number of multilateral stakeholders. In addition to the promotion of the material interests of states (often hailing from different parts of the globe), there were non-economic objectives which required care and dedication from each player. Still, some of those critical objectives were not urgent and could be allowed to move toward fruition over time, and their fulfilment would serve the interests of various parties. Nothing, however, could be really more powerful and penetrating than culture in assisting international elites to promote interconnectivity between their citizens to support these goals. Various forms of culture and cultural means could be a boon; from multinational educational programs to tourist projects and from bilingual movies and arts galleries to sports and recreation activities.

National governments were, therefore, a major force in financing a flurry of cultural programs whose prime objective was to eventually foster some degree of affinity between their own citizens and citizens of some other nations. Such projects were more successful when the participants had particular characteristics and special talents. Wider connections and lasting relationships among a higher number of capable and influential people were considered more likely to pave the ground for the creation of a friendlier environment for all stakeholders from the public and private sectors. Of course, part of the cultural endeavors supported by public funds certainly had something to do with boosting soft power so that the national political and dip-

---

276 Peter Duus, *The Abacus and the Sword: The Japanese Penetration of Korea, 1895–1910* (Berkeley: University of California Press, 1995).

lomatic goals could be secured rapidly and more effectively. Moreover, it was relatively easy to find funds for international cultural projects like these because national governments could conveniently argue that increased soft power could ultimately help them to pursue their international interests, and thus they could overcome any reticence among stakeholders from the public or private sector.

Compared to sovereign states and their official representatives, however, corporations and private businesses were more assertive in the commercialization of culture; in any event, one of the reasons national governments initiated or supported cultural programs was to promote the interests of these businesses in the first place. The danger grew when these two players worked in cahoots to take advantage of culture in favor of some remunerative financial gains.[277] As time elapsed and the interests of the business sector grew, no part of culture and cultural values was to remain sacred or immune from commodification. Everything could now be up for sale if the price tag was right.[278] Even the moral moorings and ethical principles of society could serve some crass materialistic objectives of the private sector. In particular, unscrupulous businesses actually had everything to gain and very little to lose from capitalizing on profit-generating cultural activities for the sake of promoting their interests.

Foreign Culture In Contemporary Iran

As a polyglot society and heir to multicontinental empires, Iran had long been exposed to a variety of cultural elements from many nations. Whether it was exporting or importing cultural attributes, the country had regular cultural interactions with neighboring regions. Because of its relatively large size and particular historical legacies, Iran was also a melting pot which could assimilate many cultural features of invaders. That is one reason why neither the invading armies of the Macedonian Alexander or those of the Muslim Arabs, nor the retrograde hordes of steppe Mongols and Central Asian Turks, could ultimately dominate Iranians and extirpate their lan-

---

277 Dennis L. McNamara, ed., *Corporatism and Korean Capitalism* (London and New York: Routledge, 1999); and David Hundt, *Korea's Developmental Alliance* (Abingdon and New York: Routledge, 2009), p. 25.
278 "Khoon chini dar raghay Iranian!" [Chinese Blood in the Veins of Iranians!] *Tabnak*, October 5, 2015.

guages and other aspects of cultural heritage, despite the fact that those foreign raiders occupied the country and ruled over its people for some time.[279] Quite to the contrary, the invaders themselves came to be heavily influenced by the Iranian culture and they had little option but to succumb to the cultural characteristics of Iran in order to survive in long haul.

Compared to the classical period when Persia was a leader in cultural and civilizational achievements, however, contemporary cultural interactions between Iran and some other countries, Western nations in particular, are taking place under considerably different circumstances. All of a sudden, the Iranians found themselves in a relatively weak position *vis-à-vis* their Western counterparts, politically and militarily as well as economically and technologically. For some Iranian politicians and intellectuals, the cultural and moral framework were to be blamed, partially, if not say wholly, for the perceived gap between their country and other developed societies. This was the beginning of a cultural self-mutilation which has not stopped to the present day.[280] Among the early groups of students who were sent to Europe by the Iranian government during the Qajar era (1785–1925), many returned home as promotors of Western culture and values. Moreover, the myopic books and prejudiced intellectual works which they subsequently produced greatly influenced the mindset and manners of young people in the next generations in Iran.

Under the Pahlavi dynasty (1925 until 1979), the infatuation of intellectuals with the West and their alienation from Iranian culture and traditional values reached a peak. As a corollary to that, a great number of university students and the literati practically became free agents of Western culture among their fellow citizens. They significantly influenced the mentality and behavior of many naïve and gullible young people, who more and more often chose to attend foreign universities and to travel abroad for shopping and leisure. On top of that, the political system was practically hypnotized by the West, and its diplomatic and economic policies only encouraged further penetration of Western ethics and products. Government efforts to revive the forgotten Iranian nationalism and proud history also conveniently camouflaged the quiet crusade that was being waged against the society's tradi-

279 "Persian Civilization Rich in Heritage, Culture," *Korea Times*, February 10, 2008.
280 "Chera Iran koreye jenoobi nemishavad?" [Why Doesn't Iran Become South Korea?] *Donya-e Eqtesad*, May 17, 2016.

tional customs and moral guideposts by the promotion of decadent behavior, from scenes of the royal family kissing their pet dogs (animals that many cultures consider unclean) to soft pornography.

Although the ascendancy of the Islamic Republic threw a wrench in the wheels of the Western cultural juggernaut in Iran, the penetration of foreign cultural products into the Iranian society never stopped. Anti-Americanism and a loathing of Western values were part of the official political ideology and an operational code of decision-making elites in the Islamic Republic, but Coca-Cola was produced and distributed throughout Iran, American cigarettes were imported and sold in every city and village, and recent Hollywood movies were swiftly dubbed and broadcast (after being audited and sanitized thoroughly) on national TV channels.[281] The influence of and discussions about certain Western thoughts and teachings also continued unabated in the higher education system, simply because a fair share of top academic positions were handed over to liberal and pro-Western professors. Moreover, with the growing Iranian diaspora, émigrés residing in Western countries now became another vehicle for the dissemination of certain Western ethics and manners among Iranians. Further undermining Iranian society were the sinister effects of Persian products produced by the Iranians residing abroad. In sharp contrast to the conservative fare that ordinary Iranians can find on their national TV channels, a large percentage of the songs, movies, video clips, and commercials produced by the diaspora (and broadcast through satellite channels or the internet) is laced with soft pornography and images of highly materialistic Western life-styles. New technologies further fueled the advancement of foreign cultural influence among Iranians. New communication tools were also instrumental in helping many people among the diaspora to conveniently communicate with their fellow citizens inside the country. Satellite channels, websites, and mobile phones exposed more and more impressionable Iranian youth to the influence of other cultures. Afflicted with new social and economic malaises unknown to the previous generations, this latest group of youngsters and adults were quite susceptible to the impact of cultural products coming from other territories. In this climate, foreign countries including East Asian states such as

---

281 "Iran Imports US-made Cars through South Korea," *Trend News Agency*, April 19, 2016.

South Korea could capitalize on so-called cultural diplomacy and soft power promotion in order to make headway or at least safeguard their lucrative economic interests in the Persian Gulf country.[282]

The Advent of East Asian Cultures

During the reign of the Pahlavi dynasty, Iran established cordial diplomatic and political relations with almost all East Asian countries. Besides forging bilateral connections in economic and technological fields, the two sides also signed over the years a number of formal agreements to engage in various types of cultural exchanges. However, in spite of such agreements, very little influential cultural interaction actually took place between the two sides. Language barriers as well as considerable cultural differences forestalled close and lasting cultural relations between people from the two regions,[283] which are separated from each other by many factors besides 4,000 miles of land and water. On top of that, many Iranians had become more or less obsessed with Western culture, just as was the case in some East Asian states such as Japan, South Korea, and Taiwan. It was no coincidence, therefore, that many of these people from the two sides of Asia were to sometimes learn about each other through a Western prism.

Compared to the size and scope of cultural interactions between Iran and East Asia during the Pahlavi dynasty, under the Islamic Republic the penetration of East Asian cultural products into the Iranian society reached a pinnacle. There were a number of reasons for that. First, the West and its culture had withdrawn from Iran, at least on the surface. People-to-people contacts between Iran and Western countries had greatly decreased, and fewer cultural products from the West were allowed to enter the country. The government was not interested in building a cultural relationship with Western societies, and it had even taken some official measures to curtail the emergence of such ties. Moreover, certain Western cultural materials had been declared immoral and illegal, forcing fans and importers of such goods

282 "Tehran to Host Iran–South Korea Cultural Relations Conference," *Tasnim News Agency*, April 21, 2014; "President Park Carries out Cultural Diplomacy in Qatar," *Arirang News*, March 8, 2015; "Tehran to Host Iran, S Korea Religious Dialogue," *Mehr News Agency*, January 25, 2016; "Tehran to Host Iran–Korea Joint Cultural Festival," *Tehran Times*, July 4, 2016; and "S. Korea–Iran Photo Exhibition to Open this Week," *Yonhap News Agency*, September 26, 2016.
283 Ministry of Culture and Sports, *Religious Culture in Korea* (Seoul: Ministry of Culture and Sports, Religious Affairs Office, 1996), pp. 99–100.

to think twice before making trouble for themselves. In such an environment, cultural products from Eastern countries had a far better chance to survive and flourish in Iran.

The second reason was that the cultural codes preached by the Islamic Republic had a lot in common with Iran's traditional values and morals. The institution of the family was particularly regarded as a cornerstone of a healthy and moral society, while illicit and proscribed relations between the sexes were considered a serious threat to the foundations of family and public ethics. Alcohol production and consumption were systematically banned, laws banning prostitution were reliably enforced, and any images or symbols of nudity or sexuality were pushed into the private sphere. Many cultural products produced in the West, therefore, might come into conflict with these moral codes. But unlike most of the cultural commodities from Western societies, cultural products from the East were unlikely to conflict with what the Islamic Republic considered acceptable and legitimate. In fact, there were some East Asian cultural products which the government found very useful to be presented and even promoted through the public media outlets.

Third, successive Iranian governments had to welcome some sort of cultural connections to East Asian countries in keeping with Tehran's "Look-East" policy, whose main goal was to replace the erstwhile reliance on the West for certain necessary products and services by building new connections to Eastern capitals.[284] Since Iran's relationship with the West was often chilly and even hostile, politico-economically and culturally, it had to source some of its economic and technological requirements by forging better ties with East Asia. Friendly and cordial cultural connections, no matter if sometimes pretentious and ephemeral, are usually part of government efforts to achieve political and economic objectives abroad. Any successes in Tehran's "Look-East" campaign, moreover, helped the government stand by its well-known mottos and principles with regard to Western countries, though commonly the vulnerable and susceptible segments of the citizenry had to pay the cost.

Finally, the East Asian countries themselves gradually realized that they could significantly improve their status and interests in Iran by capitalizing

---

284 "Iran's 'Look East' Partners in a Quandary," *Asia Times*, July 31, 2015.

on culture and cultural products. As compared to some Western countries, lack of soft power among the Iranian public usually hindered East Asian societies from creating better ties.[285] This was a very old hurdle which had little to do with contemporary political systems in Iran. Signing certain cultural agreements or participating in some joint cultural projects with the Iranian government could contribute to the growing interest of East Asian countries in Iran, but they badly needed to come up with other new initiatives which had the potential to inspire interest and an open attitude among the ordinary citizens.[286]

Education, entertainment, and sports are three areas where large numbers of young people can be influenced. Their inclination to instant infatuation with all sorts of things can directly translate into attachment to, and fondness for, the source country that generated those things in the first place. Among all East Asian countries, however, the ROK emerged to gain the most by far from extending cultural ties with Iran.[287]

Iranian–Korean Cultural Exchanges in Contemporary History

Tehran and Seoul signed a Treaty of Friendship during an official visit to the ROK by the Iranian Foreign Minister Ardeshir Zahedi in May 1969. This was the first time the two counties had formally signed an agreement since they established official diplomatic ties in 1962.[288]

The measure later led to various cultural interactions between Iran and South Korea, particularly in sports and education.[289] A number of friendly soccer matches were arranged between the national teams of Iran and the

285 "Korean Drama Boom in Iran to Create Business Opportunities," *Korea Times*, February 22, 2016; "Park Becomes Publicist-in-chief for S. Korean Culture in Iran," *Yonhap News Agency*, May 3, 2016; and "Park's Approval Rating Moves up after Visit to Iran," *Korea Herald*, May 5, 2016.
286 "Seoul Strives to Enhance Ties with Tehran," *Korea Herald*, September 7, 2015; and "Ambassador: Park's Visit to Iran will Definitely Deepen Ties," *Tehran Times*, April 27, 2016, pp. 1, 2.
287 "Iran–South Korea Friendly Match Set for October 18," *Tasnim News Agency*, July 30, 2014; and "Iran's Economic Relations with East Asia," *Press TV*, May 11, 2016.
288 The treaty actually made many Koreans thrilled and upbeat about potential positive implications of the measure. The *Korea Herald*, for instance, highly praised the move through publishing a flattering editorial in which the national daily stated rather effusively that "all concerned authorities and diplomats who have made the conclusion of this significant treaty with Iran a reality deserve our hearty commendation and thanks." Cited from: "Korea–Iran Amity," *Korea Herald*, May 6, 1969, p. 2.
289 "Korea to Travel to Iran for Friendly in November," *Korea Herald*, July 30, 2014; and "Iran to Play South Korea in Friendly," *Tasnim News Agency*, July 28, 2014.

ROK, while high profile academic delegates from both sides found propitious occasions to visit each other for educational or other purposes.[290] Other bilateral exchanges made by political and economic officials sometimes spawned further cultural initiatives between Tehran and Seoul. As a case in point, the inauguration of the Korean–Iranian Friendship Association (KIFA) took place when Jafar Sharif-Emami, president of the Senate of Iran and prime minister of Iran in 1960–1961, visited Seoul in July 1978.

Of all the cultural schemes launched between South Korea and Iran during the Pahlavi dynasty, however, probably none was as enduring as the twin city project. The idea of sisterhood between Seoul and Tehran, which was proposed initially by the Koreans through the Seoul Metropolitan Government in 1976, eventually made it possible for the two big cities to exchange names in 1977, each one naming a street for the other political capital. This move was unprecedented in South Korea's relationship with the entire Middle East region, and the initiative has remained an allegorical edifice of cultural connections between the ROK and Iran.

In particular, the names of both streets continued to play a role, often invisibly, when the two states were not on good terms with each other, economically and especially politically. They contributed to such a function in spite of the fact that over time, "Teheran-ro" or "Tehran Street" in Seoul grew in stature to become one of the wealthiest and most prestigious streets in the entire Korean Peninsula, while its sister in Tehran, "Seoul Street," did not really develop much, compared to many other routes and roadways in the northern part of the Iranian capital.[291]

Following the collapse of the Pahlavi monarchy and the ascendance of the Islamic Republic in 1979, cultural interactions between Iran and South Korea were negatively affected for some time. Partly this can be attributed to the fact that the two countries did not have bilateral diplomatic ties at the ambassadorial level for close to a decade throughout the 1980s. This was also a peculiar period when Iran was heavily preoccupied with its ongoing military conflict with the neighboring country, Iraq. Both problems influ-

---

290 "Russian Arrives here as Iran Soccer Coach," *Korea Herald*, September 9, 1971, p. 1; and "Investment in Education Spurs Nat'l Development," *Korea Times*, January 30, 1977, p. 5.
291 "S. Korea, Iran Discuss Cultural Cooperation Ahead of Park's Trip to Teheran," *Yonhap News Agency*, April 20, 2016.

enced Tehran's interactions with the ROK in all areas, though South Korea still tried to maintain some of its ongoing connections to Iran. On top of that, during those bloody and burdensome years, of course Iran did not much engage in cultural interactions with other nations around the world — and particularly with the West, whose culture and morality were recognized as having worked to undermine Iranian society.

Under the presidency of Akbar Hashemi Rafsanjani and his successor, Mohammad Khatami, Iran became interested in forging better non-political connections to other parts of the world. Iran desperately needed some foreign assistance to dig out of the wartime rubble and move ahead with reconstruction. Rafsanjani largely focused on economic and financial exchanges with other nations, while Khatami became renowned mostly for his cultural proclivities. But neither of the two presidents made big changes in Tehran's lackadaisical cultural relationship with the East Asian countries, including South Korea.[292] As Rafsanjani had been destined to engage primarily in political and economic fronts, Khatami was expected to contribute to the important field of culture. His by-word of "dialogue among civilization" was thought to signify, first and foremost, something cultural. But this "cultural initiative" led to more contentious political debates inside and outside Iran, and its pure cultural aspect largely targeted the Western world rather than the East.

By comparison, however, out of the blue culture became a major characteristic of the Iranian–South Korean relationship under the presidency of Ahmadinejad. True, the ROK also managed to experience the pinnacle of its economic and technological interactions with Iran at that time, but nevertheless, even the Koreans were surprised to see that the presence of their culture in Iran had all of a sudden reached its acme, even before Ahmadinejad finished the first half of his two terms in office.[293]

However, rather than a fair and equal bilateral exchange between Seoul and Tehran, the cultural exchanges turned out to be predominantly a one-way business dominated by the abrupt and unanticipated upsurge of Korean

---

292 "Moj serialhay korei jadid dar rah ast," [Wave of New Korean Serials Underway] *Asr Iran,* July 22, 2015.
293 "S Korean Businesses Preparing to Flood Iran," *Mehr News Agency,* November 8, 2015; "Tycoons Rush to Iran for Business Bonanza," *Korea Herald,* May 2, 2016; and "Envoy Discusses Doing Business in Iran," *Yonhap News Agency,* June 16, 2016.

culture in Iranian society.[294] There were certainly some external and internal justifications for the new influx of Korean goods into Iran, but those factors could not have played a critical role with regard to the way Korean cultural products flooded into Iran. What then was the nature of this Korean cultural upswing in Iran and which factors truly contributed to its success?

Hallyu Makes Inroads Into Iran

The Korean wave known as Hallyu has been a real hit among tractable and impressionable youth in some parts of the world during the past decade. By and large, Hallyu products include sensational movies, historical and mythological dramas, and ritzy-glitzy songs. Out of the three categories, however, only the second group, historical and mythological dramas, eventually snuck into the life of Iranians. Before the arrival of such Hallyu shows in Iran, many Iranian families had already viewed similar products from other East Asian countries, especially Japan and China, on TV. In the 1980s and 1990s, a number of Japanese and Chinese dramas caught the attention of many Iranians. Compared to those historical dramas and movie serials produced by Japan and China, the Hallyu hits drew a larger audience in Iran, even though by that time many Iranian families had long been linked to a wide range of international satellite channels as well as high-speed computers mostly connected to the internet.[295]

"Jewel in the Palace" was the first Korean drama that piqued the interest of Iranian TV viewers across the country. The historical Hallyu serial, which won a rating of over 50 percent, also kindled curiosity about Korea and its culture. Dubbed into Persian as "Javaheri Dar Ghasr" (from "Dae Jang Geum" in Korean), the classic drama serial attracted a good number of viewers, but the actual viewing rate was far below what the Koreans claimed. The media and press in the ROK reported that the viewing rate for "Jewel in the Palace"

---

294 "Bahar ravabet chashmbadamiha ba Iran," [The Spring of Almond-eyes' Relations with Iran] *Mardom Salari*, May 2, 2016, p. 15; and "Khodahafezi ba tejarat yektarafeh Iran va koreye jenoobi," [Goodbye to Iran and South Korea's One-way Trade] *Rah Mardom Daily*, May 3, 2016, p. 5.
295 "Imagining the Korean Wave's Future in Iran," *Korea Joongang Daily*, May 2, 2016; "K-Culture Diplomacy: From São Paulo to Tehran," *The Diplomat*, May 10, 2016; and "Yonhap-IRNA Photo Exhibition in Iran Draws to Close," *Yonhap News Agency*, October 4, 2016.

in Iran was 86 percent nationwide and 90 percent in the capital, Tehran.[296] When the Hallyu drama was first aired in South Korea from September 2003 to March 2004, its average rate of viewership was 46.3 percent. It is then not clear how this humble figure doubled when its broadcast began in Iran in November 2006.

Of course, Iranians had already heard about the Asian nation and its manufactured goods, at least through occasional, and sometimes frequent, commercial advertisements that had appeared on the national TV channels since the 1990s. Many of the viewers were also regular consumers of various Korean products which had recently become available, gradually replacing the dominance of Japanese products. Still, very few of them had really experienced Korea, as compared to tens of thousands of Iranians who had worked or studied in Japan since the 1980s. Thus the success of the "Jewel in the Palace" drama, somewhat unanticipated due to this background, only augured well for a future of other Hallyu products in Iran.[297]

If "Jewel in the Palace" was a hit in Iran, the next mythological drama, "Jumong," turned out to be an absolute smash hit. In fact, it surpassed all previous East Asian movie products when it was broadcast over a national TV channel on a weekly basis.[298] Many fans who could not be home in time for the show, because of work or other obligations, were even willing to congregate in public places such as hospitals and bus or train terminals to make sure they didn't miss any part of the mythological story. "Jumong," which had been dubbed from Korean into Persian as "The Myth of Jumong," not only triumphed by capturing higher ratings in Iran than it had already won in its source country, the ROK, but the historical drama soon became a bankable business for unscrupulous opportunists in the private market who started selling selected clips or photos extracted from the Hallyu hit through

296 "Hallyue bbajin ilan," [A Fallen for Korean Wave Iran] *Dong-A Ilbo*, February 22, 2010; "S. Korea to Build K-Tower in Iran," *Korea Herald*, May 2, 2016; and "Ilan-I yeolgwanghan 'jumong'...hallyu beullu osyeon," ['Jumong'-crazed Iran...Blue Ocean of Hallyu] *Yonhap News Agency*, September 29, 2016.
297 "Korean Movies: Cultural Envoys for Iran," *Korea Times*, November 13, 2009; "Korean Drama Boom in Iran to Create Business Opportunities," *Korea Times*, February 22, 2016; "Korean Wave in Iran," *Dong-A Ilbo*, April 30, 2016; and "Coming Two Years Crucial in Spreading Korean Culture in Iran," *Yonhap News Agency*, May 10, 2016.
298 "'Jumong' ilanseo sicheongryul 60% ingi," ['Jumong' Popularity Rating in Iran 60%] *Hankyoreh*, April 29, 2009. Another Korean source has put the viewing rate of 85 percent for "Jumong" in Iran. "Guksan tambae, ilan sobija salojabda," [Korean Cigarette Catches up with Iranian Consumers] *Asia Kyungjae*, January 29, 2016.

online outlets, hard copy magazines, etc.[299] Like "Jewel in the Palace," how-ever, the success of "Jumong" in Iran was a bigger story than some ephemeral entertainment success; the underlying importance was that cultural prod-ucts such as this could certainly have other far-reaching implications within the society in large.[300]

Besides their immediate impact in promoting Korean goods, the Hallyu hits such as "Jumong" encouraged impressionable young people when mak-ing important decisions in their lives. More youngsters took an interest in taekwondo, though the popular martial art had long fascinated many others prior to the arrival of Hallyu products.[301] One other more surprising ramifica-tions was that a growing number of people spontaneously chose to pick up the Korean language as their new hobby or even their field of study, without having an inkling about what that would entail in practical terms. In the same way, an increasing number of youngsters happened to flock to the in-ternet to search for a Korean penpal, logging into chatrooms or registering at various specialized websites. The latter group were particularly prone to potential risks associated with landing in uncharted waters.[302]

How did such a significant part of the Iranian society reach this stage? How could an entertainment product, which some Korean connoisseurs had already called a lackluster, be regarded as a blockbuster in another part of the world? As a matter of fact, the success of Hallyu in Iran surprised a lot of Ko-rean people, many of whom were impressed that their country had "scored" such an achievement in a foreign land with contrasting cultural character-istics as well as dissimilar politico-economic settings. But the instant con-quest by Korean cultural products must have been fueled by something be-yond the obvious. Was there not something strange, if not suspicious, about this type of "cultural exchanges" between the two countries? Does this count

299 "Hoshdar Iran be kore: Varedat ra motavaghef mikonim," [Iran Warning to Korea: We Stop Imports] *Tabnak*, June 27, 2012.
300 "Daejang-geum, jumong sicheongryul 90% nara...'Iraneul yeolda'," ['Opening Iran'...the Country Where 90% Watched Daejang-geum and Jumong] *Yonhap News Agency*, April 29, 2016.
301 "Iran Wins Asian Taekwondo Championships," *Press TV*, May 28, 2014; and "Tehran, Seoul to Expand Bilateral Ties: Korean Official," *Tasnim News Agency*, June 27, 2015.
302 "In Iran, Booming Korean Culture Leads Many Youngsters to Study the Language," *Korea Herald*, May 5, 2016; "In Taekwondo, South Korea and Iran are Friendly Rivals," *Yonhap News Agency*, May 10, 2016; and "Korean Contest Winner in Iran Says TV Dramas Led her to Learn Language," *Korea Times*, July 8, 2016.

as a genuinely cultural activity in the first place? If not, which factors contributed most to the publicity and popularity of Hallyu dramas in Iran over a relatively short time span? Who were the key players behind a national campaign for the promotion of a certain Korean cultural product among the Iranian citizens? What was really at stake?

Twisting Long-Lasting Realities For Instant Interests

By and large, Hallyu products can be categorized into three types. The first group consists of movies and dramas which essentially focus on some catchy aspects of daily life in modern Korea. The second type involves serials and movies devoted to historical and mythological narratives. The third class includes the catchy songs and pop music, which again reflect something of present-day life in South Korea. There are, however, other types of artistic works produced in the ROK that can be connected closely to genuine Korean folklore tales and classical music, but these usually humble and less-known items hardly ever make inroads into the mainstream domestic market, let alone foreign markets. However, despite their differences, the three types of Hallyu shows usually share certain characteristics which play a very significant role in their wide popularity.

The Hallyu movies and dramas are basically soap operas. Supposedly set in modern-day Korea, they generally present a rather different picture from the common reality that its citizens experience. These artistic productions mostly focus on the supposed ideals and behaviors of a tiny minority that has greatly benefited from the East Asian country's recent spurts of industrialization and economic development. Their stories generally illustrate the fancy lifestyles of people who have a lot of ready cash, live in commodious houses furnished with all the trappings of luxury, buy expensive brands, are frequently found planning their next exotic foreign trip, and are obsessed with some new love experience or broken relationship.[303] Such fanciful narratives of Korean life, of course, fascinate youngsters and even many adults who wish they could indulge similar habits and lifestyles, whether they are in Korea or elsewhere.

---

303 Martin Hemmert, *Tiger Management: Korean Companies on World Markets* (Abingdon and New York: Routledge, 2012), pp. 65, 77, 81.

Those serials and movies which touch upon legendary heroes and historical narratives are hardly free from the same distortions. They may range from historical dramas to historical fiction. Their stories are sometimes pure fantasy and magnified mythology, while some degree of misrepresentation or warped content is common in Hallyu products, even when they purport to present a realistic picture of various absorbing developments that occurred in ancient times. In some Hallyu of that genre, the imagined historical heroes may engage in astounding jujitsu-style fighting against the enemy or demonstrate divine powers and immortality; they know no logical boundary. Such problems may not be easily detected by naïve fans and viewers; few people have any idea of Korea's real history and its ancient mythological tales. Moreover, patriotic attitudes and nationalist sentiments incline at least many Koreans to turn a blind eye to any inaccuracies or exaggerations.

Meanwhile, a very common characteristic of nearly all Hallyu products is the altered appearance of their players. As a home for the bustling business of plastic surgery and a heavyweight in that field, regionally and internationally, South Korea as a society seems obsessed with tactics such as cosmetic surgery in the endless struggle for personal fulfilment and social achievement.

As a corollary to this atypical phenomenon, the Korean movie-making industry is replete with female and male players who have already experienced the knife of different cosmetic surgeons at least two or three times. In fact, it is almost impossible to find any Hallyu product whose main actors have not reshaped their nose or eye size at least by undergoing a type of cosmetic operation in Seoul. When a large group of such cosmetic-savvy characters appears in a movie project, they certainly give a thoroughly different impression of the country and culture they represent, no matter whether their foreign audience is already familiar with the inconvenient reality of Korean society so skillfully re-packaged for them by the Hallyu shows.[304]

Considering the Hallyu products which have so far been broadcast and promoted in Iran, nevertheless, the foregoing feature is less noticed and even hardly debated by either the public or professionals in the entertainment industry. A big reason is that only movies and dramas with historical themes

---

304 "Korea, Iran Eye Bigger Trader in Hallyu, Health, Welfare, IT," *Korea Herald*, May 2, 2016.

have thus been presented to the Iranian audience as it is almost impossible for now to let in some other types of Hallyu shows such as the "Girls Generation" which are considered to be morally unsuited for their soaked obscene dialogues and gestures. Of course, the historical and mythological serials and movies are not totally devoid of such problem, but their contents are carefully and thoroughly audited before being broadcast through the country's public media outlets especially the national TV channels. More importantly, in this class of historical Hallyu products, the dialogues and heroic actions of players may captivate the audience so deeply that they find little chance to give a second thought about the professionally changed appearances of those performers. After all, not everyone among a captivated Iranian audience may have a relatively good understanding about some Korean facts in ancient or modern times.[305]

The Ignorance Factor: When Knowing A Little Helps Hallyu

Before it was forced to open its doors to the outside world and enjoy the benefits of modern civilization, Korea used to be called the "hermit kingdom." Besides its isolation and peculiarity, the Korean Peninsula was *terra incognita* as very few people knew much about the overall characteristics of the land and its people. The forceful opening of the Korean territory to the outside world in the late 19th and early 20th centuries did not, however, change everything swiftly, because there were still few foreigners who had a real chance to visit the place and learn about its circumstances first-hand. By and large, this trend continued even after the divided southern part of the peninsula, the ROK, embarked in earnest on an ambitious project of modernization in the early 1960s. Since late 1980s and early 1990s, South Korea has been further open for international business and tourism, but only the citizens of a few countries have demonstrated more willingness to go to the place, no matter for a temporary stint as a tourist or for a longer sojourn as an English teacher or businessman.

As a corollary to that almost a bulk of the world's population has remained rather ignorant or ill-informed about what is really going on in the southern, and especially northern, part of the Korean Peninsula. Moreover,

---

305 "Ki-moon: Geneva 2 Sound Way to Solve Crisis in Syria, Talks Should Continue," *Fars News Agency*, February 19, 2014; and "Maskan korei' dar rah ast," ['Korean Housing' is Coming] *Tabnak*, October 29, 2015.

few unbiased and unprejudiced books and reports have so far been published about the real circumstances of the peninsula. On top of that, there has been a rather unhealthy assertiveness in both influential international media and powerful policy circles over the past two decades to constantly promote South Korea as a stellar experience and a successful model for emulation by other countries. As a consequence, therefore, many problems as well as shortcomings of the tiny East Asian nation have been largely eclipsed by such myopic marketing about the recent story of Korean industrialization and economic development. The highly politicization of the North Korean case or the production and publication of various negative and biased reports over years about the ruling class of Pyongyang have hardly damaged the vested interests of the South Korean elites either. This situation has greatly benefited the ROK's business sector and its nascent movie-making industry, represented by Hallyu, in many other parts of the world, including the Middle East.

Compared to some Western and Eastern countries, the Middle Eastern societies have been even less fortunate to learn enough about the Koreans and their society and culture. Few scholars or interested observers have emerged in the region to study Korea and its people. A great deal of all Korea-related books and reports available in the region are a rather lackadaisical translation of the materials which have already been produced and published somewhere else.[306] The average citizenry in the region, therefore, knows very little, if anything at all, about the circumstances of the Korean Peninsula or the way the Korean society functions.[307] And neither do the Koreans know more about the Middle East. As a case in point, an academic poster produced and distributed several times by a research department affiliated with the Seoul National University's School of Social Sciences in 2014 used Turkey's well-known Hagia Sophia (Ayasofya in Turkish) to symbolize Iran; an inadvertent incident which could speak volumes about the average understanding of the Korean citizenry about the region that has greatly benefited them at least since the early 1970s.

---

306 "Vaghti Jumong ostooreh mishavad!" [When Jumong Becomes Legend!] *Tabnak*, May 23, 2014.
307 "Al Jazeera Visits Korea for First Time," *Chosun Ilbo*, April 19, 2004; and "An Arab in South Korea," *Gulf News*, July 24, 2009.

In the Middle East, Iranians have particularly been exposed to various pro-Korean perspectives over the past decades. This situation seems somewhat natural as Tehran has long been keen to be in rather good terms with the elites of both Seoul and Pyongyang. Iranians have often been told many mesmerizing good things about the modernization spurts and industrialization experiences of South Korea, while the public media and influential figures or institutions have relatively shown a coy attitude to talk negatively about North Korea. As a result, many Iranian citizens have developed over years a rather positive impression about Korea and Koreans without knowing much about the seamy side of the East Asian country and its people.[308] The situation fortuitously helped a host of Korean companies to easily peddle their brands and products in the lucrative markets of Iran, while the Hallyu industry also found the Iranian environment very conducive to its hidden agenda of further assisting the chaebol in Iran like many other parts of the world.[309]

The heady optimism and sanguine attitudes of Iranians toward the tiny East Asian country turned out to be a boon serving many other Koreans as well. For instance, many officials in Iranian public institutions and national libraries have been willing in recent years to naively and easily hand over in the name of "cultural exchanges" some of the Persian Gulf country's most precious historical works and archives to a number of Korean scholars and public servants without having an inkling about the true mission and intention of those people. As many Koreans have strived hard in recent decades to consult various works and archives of other nations for their own sake of identity-building and nationalistic causes, some of them have taken advantage of a number of relevant yet very rare Iranian resources for such purposes, cherry-picking whatever could suit their own true mission and interests without even sometimes acknowledging or providing proper references to the original source or materials which they could easily get access to largely thanks to their "Korea-friendly" Iranian officials.

---

308 "Iraniha khoshtiptar az dabirkol sazman melal," [Iranians more Handsome than UN Secretary General] *Tabnak*, August 30, 2012; and "Aya bazikon korei be mardom Iran tohin kardeh ast?" [Did Korean Player Insult Iranian people?] *Asr Iran*, October 9, 2016.
309 "236 Businesspeople to Follow Park to Iran," *Korea Times*, April 27, 2016.

The "Imports Mafia" Hires the Media

The promotion and success of Korean manufactured and cultural products would not have been easily possible in Iran without fully taking advantage of the Iranian public media. As a matter of fact, few Iranian families really knew much about any Korean brand when the East Asian country's products began to surge in Iran's markets in the late 1990s and early 2000s. In those days, there happened to be incessant new advertisements for the Korean LG appeared on the national TV sometimes fifty times a day. Later, some other Korean brands such as Samsung and Hyundai joined the race by putting their own catchy advertisements on various Iranian public TV channels.[310] Such dubious promotional campaigns and peculiarly commercial advertisements for Korean products tended to be both omnipresent and unabating. It would be no exaggeration, therefore, to claim that during the past two decades Koreans brands have been actually advertised on Iranian public media more than any brand from either Western or Eastern countries.[311]

A similar story was to run through when a number of Korean cultural products and Hallyu dramas were brought into Iran about one decade ago. It was again the public media, the national TV in particular, which ran a major campaign in order to boost the popularity of Korean cultural products among ordinary Iranian citizens many of whom were, and still are, regular and faithful viewers of different public TV channels. Of course, various TV channels had an axe to grind with regard to unceasing advertisements for Korean manufactured products, but it was also a legitimate question for many TV viewers that what was really the necessity and urgency behind so much publicity and promotional maneuvers on almost all national TV programs in favor of a certain Korean drama? It was not really only about incessant and omnipresent promotion campaigns as the public TV channels used to allocate a good deal of their programs broadcasting a certain Korean serial sometimes several times a week, arranging various discussion panels about that serial, and surveying public opinions.[312]

---

310 "Hyundai Motor to Resume Export of Auto Parts to Iran in April," *Korea Herald*, March 15, 2016.
311 "Copy nashyaneh az ravesh froosh Apple dar Iran tavassot koreiha!" [Amateurish Copy of Apple Sales Method by Koreans in Iran!] *Khabar Online*, July 26, 2015.
312 "Bazar Iran, loghmei charb baray serialhay korei," [Iran Market, a Greasy Loaf for Korean Serials] *Hamseda*, April 20, 2010; and "Yek serial korei jadid dar resaneh melli," [A New Korean Serial on National Broadcaster] *Jahan News*, January 17, 2015.

Moreover, advertisements and promotional campaigns for Korean products in Iran were not constrained only to various public TV channels. There were some other public sectors which possessed similar capabilities to help promoting Korean products in the country. For instance, countless promotional venues belonging to the colossus municipality of Tehran, and many other major cities across Iran, have long played an important role in the publicity and popularity of Korean products among the Iranian citizens.[313] From running everlasting advertisements in subways to erecting giant neon sign boards throughout cities, public municipalities turned out to be another effective means to serve as a major publicity muscle of the "imports mafia" to further push Korean goods into Iran. The elephantine municipality of Tehran and its conservative mayor were even accused of betraying the national interests by going after their own selfish material interests and giving priority to the promotion of Korean goods in the so-called year of "resistance economy."

Another equally controversial issue was that Korean companies were accused that they partly financed various advertisements and commercial activities to promote the ROK's manufactured goods and Hallyu products in Iran. Such financial sponsorship could hardly surprise any concerned person as far as advertisements and publicity campaigns for various Korean brands and manufactured products in Iran were concerned. A big problem was, however, the financial role of Korean companies to help promoting certain Hallyu shows among the Iranian citizens in the name of cultural exchanges between the ROK and Iran.[314] The Koreans were alleged, for instance, that they had paid a lot of money to the public Iranian TV to broadcast some shows produced by the Hallyu industry.[315] In some other occasions, there was little doubt that Korean companies had financially sponsored a number

---

313 "Hakemiyat 'varedatchiha' bar eghtesad," [Sovereignty of 'Importers' over Economy] *Jahan News*, January 12, 2016.

314 "South Korean, Iranian Orchestras to Perform in Tehran," *Tehran Times*, April 26, 2016; "S. Korea Holds Cooking Event for Iranians," *Yonhap News Agency*, May 2, 2016; "In Tehran, 'Korea Culture Week' Receives Welcoming Response," *Yonhap News Agency*, May 3, 2016; "Iran–Korea One Heart Festival Held in Tehran," *Press TV*, May 3, 2016; and "Poets from Korea, Iran to Meet in Tehran," *Korea Herald*, April 28, 2016.

315 In fact, Koreans have brazenly taken advantage of even some natural misfortunes that befell Iranians in order to advance their commercial interests in the country through Hallyu. Iranian authorities, like many among the citizenry, are swiftly and sadly hoodwinked into such feigned maneuvers and fake gestures. See, for instance: "Lee Young-ae Donates 106 mln Won for Pohang Iran Quake Victims," *Yonhap News Agency*, November 20, 2017, and "Iran Honors Lee Young-ae for Kermanshah Quake Relief Donation," *Tehran Times*, December 15, 2017.

of cultural programs in Tehran during which they had brought in the main actors of a certain popular drama just to chat and take photos with their Iranian fans.[316]

What is still not clear is, nevertheless, whether or not the "imports mafia" and its Korean business partners have managed to sneak into some other influential public channels such as *Press TV*, which is a state-owned English language news and documentary network operating 24-hour a day, though its headquarter is based in Tehran. What is surprising is that the network has hired one, and sometimes more than one, permanent correspondent for its Seoul office, while it yet to make a similar move with regard to more important East Asian countries of China and Japan. As Iran's top trading partner and a very important political associate on the world stage, China certainly deserved a place for *Press TV*'s international activities and journalist recruitment. More recently, the public budget-financed Iranian network put on its weekly scheduled programs a broadcasting timing for a Korean documentary dubbed into English as "splendid but sad days," though it is hard to find out whether *Press TV* itself fully shouldered the bill to purchase and dub this program regardless of its quality and viewing rate.

Dreaming of A *Deus Ex Machina*

Over the past several decades, Iranian society has been in the throes of incessant politico-economic as well as socio-cultural predicaments. To top the list was the bloody Iran–Iraq War which either totally destroyed or partially damaged the lives of millions, while the internecine conflict had been destined to leave its scars on the next generations in many other different ways. The war had been ghastly and atrociously imposed upon the Iranians and they were totally hapless to do anything about it. Besides the terrible traumas of war and its repellent ramifications, an overwhelming majority of Iranian people were still had to bear with a well-coordinated international regime of sundry sanctions levied against them under one or other phony

---

316 "Korean Drama Screening Event Draws Large Number of Iranian Fans," *Yonhap News Agency*, May 3, 2016. The possibility cannot be ruled out that the Chaebol have also used popular Hallyu actors and actresses as a front in various other forms and occasions to further their interests in the Persian Gulf country. In order to make a better impression among more individuals and score larger deals in the public and private sectors, for instance, major Korean companies with a big market share in Iran could simply donate to the hapless victims of a natural disaster a few thousand dollars in care of a famous Hallyu actor or actress.

pretext.[317] The menace of war lasted about eight years, but the protracted regime of cruel sanctions was to never come to an end, taking its great toll on large swathes of ordinary citizens who were both clueless and powerless about their humiliated country and its abundant ruined opportunities.[318]

Another equally detrimental affliction was the mass exodus of the country's best and brightest human resources whose inconceivable loss turned out to be one of the greatest tragedies in the entire long history of Iran. No less than ten percent of the whole population departed the country over a course of some three and half decades; a sobering episode that gave rise to an incomprehensible phenomenon of Iran's brain drain, beauty drain, and capital drain, all of which significantly depleted the ancient country of a number of pivotal sources of power and prosperity. It is not really that hard to figure out what happens when a country loses millions of its best people.[319] Although Iranians could certainly rebuild the rubble of the war, over time, and come up with policies and tactics sooner or later to partially alleviate various injuries inflicted by the savage economic sanctions since the early 1980s, there could hardly be any remedy or replacement for the pitiful loss of so many talented and resourceful people. This mass migration had negative reverberations that will endure for many generations to come.[320]

The foregoing maladies were not certainly the only nefarious infections the Iranians had to put up with, but those plagues inevitably afflicted the country in many ways particularly economically and socially. From skyrocketing inflation to unprecedented levels of mass unemployment among the educated youth and from high rates of divorce to mind-blowing numbers of drug addicts among teenagers, the Iranian society was indubitably under-

---

317 Eyler, pp. 44, 51, 186.
318 "Iranians Were Real Victims of Western Sanctions," *International Business Times*, May 9, 2014; "Iran's Two-Decade Collapse in Prosperity," *Bloomberg*, July 10, 2015; and "Legacy of Iran–Iraq War Lives on," *BBC*, October 5, 2015.
319 "Iranian Brian Drain Looks Likely to Continue," *AFP*, June 1, 2005; "Huge Cost of Iranian Brain Drain," *BBC*, January 8, 2007; "2 hezar milyard dollar sarmayeh Iranian kharejneshin," [$2,000 Billion Wealth of Expatriate Iranians] *Asr Iran*, June 13, 2015; and "Rotbeh nakhost Iran dar farar maghzha," [Iran Number One in Brain Drain] *Tabnak*, November 17, 2015.
320 "Brain Drain Blights Iran's Economy as Investors Wait in Wings," *Bloomberg*, April 28, 2014, "Amid Iranian 'Brain Drain,' President Rouhani Congratulates Iran-born Fields Medal Winner," *Washington Post*, August 13, 2014; and "Khorooj 50 milyard dollar ba mohajerat tahsilkardegan," [Migration of Educated People Drains $50 Billion] *Tabnak*, August 23, 2014.

going a very chaotic period.[321] As a corollary to this, a hobby horse among many people, from elderly to youngsters, was to always keep talking and discussing about their unwanted problems and anxieties. They were essentially wondering how things ended up like this and why a land of permanent plenty became a laboratory of perpetual perturbation.[322] The younger generation blamed the older generation, and by doing so both of them critically failed to grasp the genesis of the crisis. After all, only a righteous sense of unfairness and victimhood or an injudicious discharge of anxiety and consternation were no good panacea to the society's chronic ills and sobering misfortunes.[323]

Instead of dealing with the national crisis rationally and coming up with practical solutions to partially chip away at various knotty problems the society was encountering, nonetheless, many people used to often ask for the divine providence to intervene in their favor. The longer they found themselves hapless with regard to their failures and troubles, the louder they wished for a celestial savior to come to the rescue. Since their country had long been a cradle of stouthearted heroes and world-class conquerors, there was surely nothing wrong in expecting one of them to resurface and out of the blue make all their wishes come true. This burgeoning desire for a champion or rescuer helped make some Korean historical dramas swiftly succeed with Iranian audiences. Prior to the arrival of the Korean wave in Iran, a number of similar shows from other East Asian countries such as Japan and China had also infatuated many Iranian viewers, giving credence to the assertion that the society is still a right target for artistic productions which deal with chivalry and heroism of an approving genre.

Among all Korean dramas and serials which were broadcast in Iran, therefore, none of them could evoke such chivalrous sentiment among the public than "Jumong." For many Iranians, the Hallyu drama had skillfully

321 "Iranian Asylum-seeker Beaten to Death: Australian Review," *Global Post*, May 26, 2014; and "Iran Executed All Adult Men in One Village for Drug Offences, Official Reveals," *Guardian*, February 26, 2016.
322 "Iran's Out of Control Kidney Bazaar," *National Review Online*, August 9, 2014; "Iran's Next Need: Internal Healing," *New York Times*, July 21, 2015; and "Sarmayehgozari Samsung baray takhrib asar tarikhi Tehran," [Samsung Investment for Destroying Historical Sites of Tehran] *Memari News*, July 24, 2015.
323 "Money Can Buy Anything in Iran, Says Ex-police Chief," *Telegraph*, June 15, 2015; "Tabagheh motavasset dar Iran az bein rafteh ast," [Middle Class in Iran Wiped Out] *Tabnak*, December 15, 2015; and "Marijuana Use is Rising in Iran, With Little Interference," *New York Times*, June 26, 2016, p. A10.

been made to conjure up their aspiration for a hero who could courageously fight for a noble cause and ultimately win over any sort of insurmountable hurdle. By watching every episode of the serial for about an hour on a weekly basis, many interested viewers could at least overlook their own life troubles fleetingly, hoping that one day a Jumong-style legendary figure will emerge and eventually turn the pages to their liking. That is one reason why "Jumong" became highly popular more among ordinary and unfeigned people in small towns and local suburbs than many rich and highly educated classes in swanky and affluent areas of the capital and other major cities. Moreover, "Jumong" became for sometimes a leitmotiv among some of those intrigued fans who hardly failed dreaming for an analogous scenario in which a plucky champion and a lionhearted national hero miraculously transform the whole system and rearrange the state of affairs to their favor.[324]

An Unsung Contribution of the Persian Language

For more than half a century, the business of dubbing foreign movies into Persian has played a big part in smoothing the way for various foreign cultures to make inroads into the Iranian society. Although people have often been struck by the success of certain foreign cultural products, in particular those related to the entertainment industry, little thought has been given to how the Persian language may be facilitating these successes. Persian has been instrumental in exposing the Iranian society to millions of written works produced in foreign languages over the past century. As in the entertainment industry, foreign authors, and sometimes their Iranian translators, have received almost all the credit for any success and popularity scored by a foreign work, while the influential component of the Persian language behind such accomplishments has largely been taken for granted.[325]

The boom of dubbed Hallyu products in recent years in Iran, therefore, has also had something to do with the power of the Persian language which functions as a fulcrum behind the country's thriving movie-making industry. Despite its structural problems, this growing Iranian entertainment field has actually obtained significant international fame over the past years by

---

324 "Safir koreye jenoobi: Kore faghat Jumong va Jang-geum nist," [South Korean Ambassador: Korea is not Only about Jumong and Jang-geum] *Tabnak*, May 1, 2016.
325 "Kari ke 'Jumong' baray kore kard," ['Jumong' Service to Korea] *Tabnak*, July 10, 2016.

grabbing various high-profile and outstanding prizes awarded to its directors and screenwriters as well as actors and actresses. In fact, the Iranian movie-making business itself is yet to deservedly acknowledge the effective element of Persian in making easier for the industry to market its products both nationally and internationally. The people involved in a movie or serial receive a lion's share of all praises and prizes, while the role of their spoken national language is as usual ignored. But what are some advantages of the Persian language which help both national and international cultural products to capture the attention of more intrigued people among their Iranian viewers and fans?

First, Persian is an old language and its rich and resourceful vocabulary has huge potential for helping screenwriters and directors to produce creative and entertaining movies and dramas. Not only can such an attribute be a forceful factor in translating and interpreting written and audio works from other languages, it easily accelerates the task of those people who engage in the business of dubbing movies and dramas from other tongues into the Persian language. Moreover, Persian has more sounds than some other languages, which makes it easier to dub a work into Persian than into some foreign tongues. This problem is particularly compelling with regard to the national languages spoken by the Northeast Asian nations of China, Korea, and particularly Japan. Because of such ingrained feature, various artistic works which have so far been dubbed from those Asian languages into Persian have been relatively successful and popular with their Iranian audience.[326]

Besides its own potential, moreover, Persian benefits from many other Iranian languages and dialects which have considerably enriched it in one way or another. As a polyglot society, Iran has historically been a land of many languages and cultures all of which have greatly contributed to its inherited civilization and shared identity. In order to fully take advantage of such huge cultural wealth, therefore, it is often very common for an Iranian movie director to tap into various languages and dialects spoken in Iran while producing a new artistic work. Additionally, a similar strategy has sometimes been applied by Iranian companies which have dubbed into the Persian language a

---

326 "Dubleh asar korei sakhttar ast," [Dubbing Koreans Works is Tougher] *Mehr News Agency*, October 7, 2015.

movie or drama from other tongues, even when the original work had been produced using only one language or only one single dialect. This approach has certainly been very effective in promoting a certain foreign movie or serial among various Iranian ethnicities whose affiliated language or local dialect had something to contribute to the final dubbed version.

Finally, the dubbed Hallyu products, like a number of other foreign works, had become really entertaining for many Iranian viewers because they used lots of humorous and witty material borrowed from Persian. After all, almost all historical Korean dramas are particularly famous for their monotonous polite language and highly formal dialogues. But it makes a big difference when parts of such rather stiff and dull artistic works are converted into other languages such as Persian by re-recording ceremonious conversations with casual dialogues and by mixing courteous expressions with witty and humorous insertions. Such a dubbed work may become even more interesting to its potential viewers when the re-voicing process involves several languages or dialects simultaneously. This is one reason why some pundits used to argue that the Hallyu products would have had a very little chance to succeed in Iran if they had been broadcast in their original Korean language, even when a great number of their Iranian viewers could supposedly understand the rather tough tongue of the East Asian nation.[327]

Other Influential Elements

In recent years, various top universities and high-profile research centers in Iran have conveyed many development-related national or international conferences and seminars during which the Korean industrialization experience has often been one of the hot topics discussed by the people involved. Moreover, a growing number of experts have written more favorably on the subject, boosting the East Asian country's overall cultural image among many Iranian citizens. A number of those specialists and commentators have sometimes written or talked very positively by accentuating only well-known good points and glossing over the seamy side of the Korean modernization story. Since some of them often wield significant authority over their audience, what they delivered could still considerably shape the mindset of

327 "Chera serialhay korei tarafdar darand?" [Why Are Korean Serials Popular?] *Jahan News*, July 29, 2015.

many people no matter if they themselves had never experienced the Asian country firsthand.[328]

Of course, the Iranian media and foreign reporters both disseminated a certain interpretation of the Korean industrialization and development experience.[329] For their part, the media and press disseminated a flurry of catchy materials prepared by their journalists and editorial departments. [330] The private sector and the "imports mafia" sometimes played a role, too, but not everything produced and promulgated by the media had been influenced by outside forces.[331] There are simply some journalists and commentators whose positive opinion about the Korean narrative has determined the way they have covered the East Asian nation and its recent cultural influence in Iran.[332] Favorable viewpoints expressed by experts and pundits as well as approving judgements made by the media and press, therefore, have encouraged more of the citizenry to enthusiastically flock to the TV rooms and watch a new series of another Korean drama. The enthusiasm of some officials in the two countries to promote the application of more newfangled "cultural technologies" would certainly encourage more Iranians to watch the Hallyu products.[333]

Last but not least, the diplomatic missions stationed in Tehran and Seoul have been effective in promoting this. Of course, official representatives and political agents are generally supposed to do their utmost when it comes to both securing and promoting their home country's interests in a host country. An important part of their mission would be to focus on promoting culture. They may also take advantage of non-cultural events or activities organized somewhere in the host country in order to give publicity to certain characteristics of their own cultural heritage. While people working at Iranian and Korean diplomatic missions have undoubtedly been cognizant of

---

328 "Toseh koreye jenoobi va darshay an baray Iran," [South Korean Development and Its Lessons for Iran] *Tabnak*, January 29, 2014.
329 "Iran to Publish Title on Tehran–Seoul Relations," *Iran Book News Agency (IBNA)*, November 27, 2013.
330 "150 Foreign Media Active in Iran," *Mehr News Agency*, June 27, 2016.
331 "Eshteghalzae barjam amma baray kharejiha," [Job Creation through the JCPOA but for Foreigners] *Javan*, November 22, 2016, pp. 1, 4.
332 "Korean Cultural Festival Bringing More Pleasant Autumn to Tehran," *Tehran Times*, September 26, 2016, pp. 1, 16.
333 "Seoulseo 'han-ilan munhwa kisul poleom'," [Seoul to Host 'Korea–Iran Cultural Technology Forum'], *Yonhap News Agency*, August 29, 2017.

this responsibility, it seems that the Koreans have been far more successful at least in the area of culture promotion in Iran.

Even when the ROK first established its Tehran embassy in April 1967, the Korean ambassador used to mail to Seoul reports about his host country covering everything from the size of the harvest and the price of melons and tomatoes to diplomatic meetings and political rumors. Since then, the ROK's envoys have hardly missed any opportunity in Iran to win an economic contract for Korean companies or to score a political advantage for their own country.[334] The East Asian country's diplomatic mission in Tehran has also been like a second home for its diaspora community in Iran, hosting CEOs of Korean companies to share business tips and legal consultations as well as receiving ordinary Korean students for educational guidance and cultural counselling. In recent years, the embassy has been more active in the area of culture promotion besides its politico-diplomatic and economic endeavors. From lobbying Iran's top university to launch a Korean studies program to sponsoring informal meetings to cater to the top actor of a Hallyu drama in Tehran, the embassy has played an active role in the promotion and success of Korean culture in the Persian Gulf country.[335]

In sharp contrast to the Korean embassy in Tehran, the Iranian embassy in Seoul seems to have done more to promote the culture of its host country than its own. As a case in point, for several years the embassy organized big parties to celebrate Nowruz, the Iranian new year (conventionally in late March), at a rather expensive hotel in Seoul — an event to which popular Korean actors and actresses were invited as honorary guests.[336] Instead of inviting Iranian celebrities or promoting the Iranian culture at those special meetings, therefore, the embassy spent its publicly-financed budget to cater to the interests of Korean culture — a wasted opportunity at best, and an ill-advised and injudicious activity.[337] On top of that, the embassy hires an

---

334 "Iran, Greater Future Opportunity," *Korea Times*, February 10, 2008; and "Korea to Build K-Tower in Iran," *Korea Herald*, May 2, 2016.
335 "The Future of Iran–South Korea Relations Is Bright: Analyst," *Tehran Times*, July 15, 2016.
336 "Jumong mihman jashn Nowrouz," [Jumong Guest of Nowrouz Celebration] *Tabnak*, March 25, 2014; and "Lee Young-ae Celebrates Iranian New Year," *Chosun Ilbo*, March 24, 2015.
337 "S Korea Eng. Society Awards Iran Envoy for Intl. Coop.," *Mehr News Agency*, April 2, 2016; and "Koreiha dar Iran sad va nirougah misazand," [Koreans to Build Dam and Power Plant in Iran] *Tafahom*, May 1, 2016, p. 3.

increasing number of Korean nationals and this misguided policy makes the place seem like a typical Korean environment, even for those Seoul-based Iranians who need to drop by the diplomatic mission to sort out their business or consular affairs.[338]

Prospects of Korean Culture In Iran

During Park Geun-hye's visit to Iran, she and her counterparts agreed to host a "Year of Korea–Iran Cultural Exchanges" in both countries, scheduled for 2017. The two governments also reached an agreement to set up a Korean cultural center in Tehran in order to lay the groundwork for various bilateral linkages that would foster this as-yet largely undeveloped area of cooperation. The new approach of the ROK government signifies that Korea is pleased with the success of its Hallyu products in Iran over the past years and hopes that fresh investments in cultural activities will continue to create a favorable environment for its massive economic machine as it continues to penetrate Iran one way and another. Moreover, Korea's relative cultural success in Iran has convinced them that the country has a huge potential, at least in the wider Middle East region, to make inroads through "cultural diplomacy" and "soft power" on a larger scale.[339]

Contrary to such upbeat assumptions and cheerful expectations, however, Iranian society has been voicing more and more discontent with what seems to be an unfair and largely one-sided promotion of Korean culture in the country.[340] For instance, religious leaders and heads of various theology schools have repeatedly warned against the negative ramifications of broadcasting Hallyu soap operas, which cannot avoid influencing the citizenry's cultural mores and social ethics — though the dubbed Korean shows had already assuredly been sanitized of any sexual scene or immoral talk.[341] Art-

338 "Lee Young-Ae Invited to "Nowruz" Hosted by Iranian Envoy," *The Seoul Times*, March 22, 2015; and "Lee Young-ae Celebrates Iranian New Year," *Chosun Ilbo*, March 24, 2015.
339 "Korea Agro-Fisheries & Food Trade Corp. Focuses on Halal," *Business Korea*, May 22, 2015; "Iran, South Korea to Hold Policy Talks this Week," *Tasnim News Agency*, June 10, 2015; and "Iran, South Korea to Focus on Establishing Mutual Cultural Centers: Official," *Tehran Times*, October 3, 2016.
340 "Empratoori Jumong va doostan dar television!" [The Empire of Jumong and Friends in Television!] *Mehr News Agency*, January 19, 2015.
341 "Enteghad emamjomeh Tuyserkan az pakhsh filmhay korei dar seda va sima," [Tuyserkan's Friday Prayer Imam Criticizes Broadcasting of Korean Movies by IRIB] *Tasnim News Agency*, June 9, 2014.

ists, performers and entertainers and those associated broadly with the Iranian movie-making industry are also discontented.[342] Drawing comparisons with Iran's own internationally-acclaimed artistic productions, many actors and directors have raised professional questions about the rationale behind allocating so much time and resources on national TV channels to Korean serials.[343] They also cautioned the government's cultural authorities not to promote foreign cultural shows at the cost of Iran's own artistic products and the many dedicated artists who stand behind those works.[344]

To better understand such grievances and criticisms raised by many Iranian artists and cultural connoisseurs, a brief comparison between the ROK and Iran's movie-making industries in terms of winning prestigious international awards may reveal some points. Since 1962, South Korea has submitted movies in order to compete for the Academy Award for Best Foreign Language Film which is handed out every year by the U.S. Academy of Motion Picture Arts and Sciences. The East Asian country has so far submitted a total of twenty-nine movies for consideration by the Academy, but not even one of them has ever received an Oscar nomination.[345] As compared to South Korea, however, Iran has participated in this rather renowned and illustrious international competition regularly since 1994. Prior to that, the country had submitted only one film in 1977. Out of a total of twenty-three films which Iran has so far sent for Oscar consideration, three films (*Children of Heaven, A Separation*, and *The Salesman*) actually received an Oscar nomination. Two of the three nominated films (*A separation*, and *The Salesman*) eventually won the award.[346]

---

342 "Busan International Film Festival to Screen Iranian Film," *Press TV*, June 1, 2015.
343 "Television ba kharid serial chini va korei poolash ra door mirizad," [Television Squanders its Money by Purchasing Chinese and Korean Serial] *Mardomsalari*, July 10, 2016, p. 11.
344 "Vaghti koreiha az ab kare migirand," [When Koreans Turn Water into Butter], *Shahrvand Daily*, September 1, 2016, p. 14.
345 "Oscars: South Korea Submits 'The Throne' for Foreign-Language Category," *The Hollywood Reporter*, September 3, 2015; and "Korea Hails 'A Taxi Driver' for Oscar Race," *Variety*, September 4, 2017.
346 "Iran Wins First Oscar with 'A Separation'," *Chicago Tribune*, February 27, 2012; and "The Salesman Wins Best Foreign Language Oscar," *The Guardian*, February 27, 2017.

Table 3. Academy Awards for Best Foreign Language Film

Submitting country	Total films submitted	Total films nominated	Total winning films
Iran	23	3	2
South Korea	29	0	0

Source: *Academy Awards Database* available at awardsdatabase.oscars.org

The crux of the problem is that culture has been exploited not for its own sake but for economic interests. Koreans bears the responsibility for having given the distinct impression that it has been using cultural products and "soft power" first and foremost to promote the interests of its giant corporations in other parts of the world. This materialistic and myopic approach to sensitive cultural matters may — fleetingly — bear fruit in some foreign societies, but its success is highly doubtful in the long haul. Moreover, misunderstanding culture and abusing it for the sake of some material gains can be potentially ruinous, as it taints even the more genuine areas of high-brow cultural and people-to-people exchanges.[347] Even when culture is going to be exploited in this way, the policy needs to be implemented very vigilantly and prudently lest its target people get the impression that they are being played for fools.[348]

As a case in point, in the midst of Park's official visit to Tehran, the Korean media were talking about her "Roosari economic diplomacy" in Iran, subtly indicating that the president's choice to wear the veil was made largely to score more economic contracts rather than actually respecting Iran's customs and dress code for female foreign VIPs. Dozens of high profile female leaders from other countries visited Iran before and after Park, but none of them left this negative impression in the host country. The Korean media used the "Roosari economic diplomacy" leitmotiv to stand for Park's overall objectives in Iran in all cultural, economic, and political areas.[349]

347 "Iran, South Korea to Launch Direct Flight by Year's End," *Trend News Agency*, May 2, 2016; "Yonhap CEO in Iran to Expand News, Information Exchange," *Yonhap News Agency*, May 15, 2016; and "'Long-term Engagement Key to Investing in Iran'," *Korea Herald*, June 12, 2016.
348 "Beyond Cultural Misperceptions of the Middle East," *Korea Herald*, May 26, 2008; "Itaewon -- Where Korea Meets the Islamic World," *Korea Herald*, April 27, 2015; and "Interview with Iranian Ambassador: S. Korea, Iran to Deepen Relationship Based on Common Shared Values," *Business Korea*, June 30, 2016.
349 "Park to Wear Hijab during Iran Visit Next Month," *Korea Times*, April 23, 2016; and "President's Dress Code for Iran Visit Stirs Debate," *Korea Times*, April 29, 2016.

The future of Korean "soft power" diplomacy toward Iran, like many other nations, therefore, depends on how prepared the East Asian nation is to engage in authentic cultural undertakings and high-level people-to-people exchanges detached from materialistic motivations.[350] This kind of interaction also has to be conducted on a real two-way basis in line with the national cultural characteristics of each party. The ROK's recent push for further cultural promotion in Iran would be more effective when the programs are developed on symbiotic terms so that both societies find new opportunities to learn about each other, without being obsessed about how to make money from every encounter.[351] Genuine cultural exchanges and true reciprocity would certainly provide a better foundation for robust and durable bilateral connections in other areas. After all, cultural bonds have more potential to survive in the long run than any type of partnership sealed by momentary material interests.[352]

North Korean Cultural Presence in Iran

Compared to the performances and shows produced by or associated with South Korea, North Korea is practically invisible in Iran. In spite of the talk and international publicity about close cooperation between the DPRK and the Islamic Republic, Iranians have hardly been offered a chance to personally experience any element of North Korean culture. Few Iranians have ever seen a dubbed North Korean movie or drama broadcast by a major national TV channel. Nor can many of them have been to a concert hall to listen

350 "Iran, S Korea Call for Ties Beyond Trade," *Mehr News Agency*, June 28, 2015; "Iran, S Korea Sign MoU on Lab Coop.," *Mehr News Agency*, July 13, 2015; "Iran, S Korea to Build Power Plant in Chabahar," *Mehr News Agency*, September 9, 2015; "Iran–South Korea Ties Can Promote Global Peace: Rouhani," *Press TV*, November 7, 2015; and "Iran, S Korea to Boost Academic Coop.," *Mehr News Agency*, October 19, 2016.

351 "Iran, South Korea Discuss Expansion of Ties," *Fars News Agency*, November 18, 2013; "Iran, South Korea to Enhance Maritime Cooperation," *Fars News Agency*, March 10, 2014; "Iran, S. Korea Keen to Strengthen All-Out Relation," *Fars News Agency*, August 19, 2014; "Companies Urged to Invest in 'Open Door' Iran," *Korea Joongang Daily*, September 17, 2015; "Iran, S Korea Launch Shipbuilding Coop.," *Mehr News Agency*, December 5, 2015; "Iran, South Korea to Establish Joint Trade Desk," *Mehr News Agency*, September 24, 2016; and "Iran, S. Korea to Boost Economic Relations," *Tasnim News Agency*, September 24, 2016.

352 "Iran, South Korea Keen to Expand Ties," *Fars News Agency*, May 2, 2014; "Iran, S. Korea to Boost Economic Ties," *Mehr News Agency*, August 23, 2015; "S. Korea Impatient to Invest in Iran: FM," *Tasnim News Agency*," November 8, 2015; and "Iran, Korea Eye Cooperation in Petrochemical Field," *Trend News Agency*, August 2, 2016.

to an orchestra of traditional Korean music from Pyongyang. It is also un-likely that any national or local museums in Iran have held exhibits of North Korean artifacts. Scientific, educational, and cultural exchanges involving Iranian and North Korean academic bodies and research institutions, too, have yet to get off the ground.[353]

Of course, Iranian and North Korean officials from different ministries and cultural bodies have signed dozens of agreements since the early 1970s in order to foster cultural interchanges between the two parties.[354] But the problem is that such bilateral accords and agreements have either been shelved somewhere or they have been implemented only partially and tem-porarily, for whatever reason. It is hard to claim that the two countries have good cultural relations when only their national soccer or swimming teams have faced each other during international or regional sports competitions hosted by Iran, North Korea, or a third country. Moreover, just about the only time North Korea is mentioned on an Iranian national TV channel is when Tehran runs a report about the contemporary international contro-versy over the North Korean nuclear issue.[355] Thus, there is no "cultural ex-change" *per se* going on between Iran and the DPRK.

Where they do have well-established relations is at the level of political culture, and this has played an important role, as exhibited largely in three different forms since the early 1980s. First, many Iranian and North Korean officials have long underscored their shared political cultural attitudes and united policies vis-à-vis certain foreign powers and rival ideologies. During various high profile diplomatic meetings as well as on the sidelines of many regional and international forums and seminars, therefore, the two sides have accentuated the existence of a common political culture between both soci-eties by pointing to their persistent and uncompromising resistance against the powers which have always tried to harm them in one way or another.[356]

353 "Iran, North Korea Vow to Bolster Ties," *Fars News Agency*, October 7, 2013; "The Hidden North Korea–Iran Strategic Relationship," *Washington Times*, March 30, 2016.
354 "Iranian Women Volleyball Squad Routs N. Korea," *Mehr News Agency*, September 4, 2016.
355 Paul French, *North Korea: The Paranoid Peninsula – A Modern History*, second edition (London and New York: Zed Books, 2007), p. 211.
356 "Sanad hamkari moshtarek bein Iran va koreye shomali emza shod," [Joint Cooperation Document Signed between Iran and North Korea] *Mehr News Agency*, September 1, 2012.

This declared solidarity has also been a leitmotiv of successive North Korean ambassadors to Tehran who, in interviews and speeches, have highlighted time and again a shared political culture between the DPRK and Iran.[357]

Second, many among the educated and literate class of Iranians have attempted to repudiate the shared political culture asserted to exist between their own people and North Koreans. This attitude is often in sharp contrast with the foregoing orientation which has usually been echoed by officials in diplomatic and policymaking circles.[358] Moreover, such a perspective has emphasized the differences between Iranian and North Korean political cultures by scrutinizing the ways the societies differ in all political, economic and cultural realms.[359] Despite acknowledging certain commonalities between the political ideologies and international rhetoric of the DPRK and the Islamic Republic over the past three and half decades, nevertheless, this nonpartisan and unprejudiced stance has found very little to affirmatively recognize as a common political culture involving Iranian and North Korean citizens.[360]

Third, many local Iranian communities and grassroots groups across the country have voiced a clear disinclination to have a North Korean-style political culture.[361] This aversion has sometimes been stressed through clear-cut mottoe such as "Iran is not North Korea," "Tehran and Pyongyang are worlds apart," "we don't want to be another North Korea," and "we would

---

357 "Taraghi dar didar ba safir jadid korye shomali: Moghavemat mardom korye shomali dar moghabel tahrimha ra setayesh mikonim," [Taraghi in Meeting with North Korean New Ambassador: We Praise North Korean People's Stand against Sanctions] *Mizan Online News Agency*, January 17, 2015; "Darkhast gheirmotaaraf va gheirghanooni America baray ghateh ravabet Iran va korye shomali," [American Unconventional and Unlawful Request for Rupturing Relations between Iran and North Korea] *Islamic Consultative Assembly News Agency*, June 28, 2016; and "Davat korye shomali az Iran baray moghableh ba America," [North Korea Invites Iran to Stand up to the United States] *Iranian Students' News Agency*, October 16, 2017.
358 "Naghdi bar moghayeseh Iran va korye shomali," [A Criticism on Comparing Iran and North Korea] *Tejarat News*, September 3, 2017.
359 "Do morabbi az koreye shomali haft mah Judo Iran ra sarekar gozashtand," [Two Trainers from North Korea Hoodwinked Iranian Judo for Seven Months] *Tabnak*, July 22, 2014.
360 "Darkhast koreye shomali az helal ahmar Iran: Be ma komak konid," [North Korea's Request from Iranian Red Crescent: Help us] *Asr Iran*, July 1, 2015.
361 "Yek mizbani vizhe be neshan 'koreye shomali nashodan'," [A Special Host for 'Not Becoming North Korea'] *Asr Iran*, April 27, 2016; and "Nabayad koreye shomali ra olgoo garardad," [North Korea Should Not be Taken as a Role Model] *Arman Daily*, August 6, 2016, p. 1.

risk being a second North Korea if we followed that policy." Deep down, Iranians have generally been quite reluctant to be compared to the reclusive East Asian country.[362] The globetrotting Iranian diaspora, which influences people inside the country in different ways, has been even more unwilling to have anything to do with the North Korean political culture. All such impediments have weighed upon any attempt to facilitate real cultural exchanges between Iran and North Korea despite more than half a century of official diplomatic relations.[363]

362 "The Iran Pact Is Not a Model for Dealing with Reclusive North Korea," *Radio Free Asia*, April 15, 2015; "False Comparison of N. Korea to Iran, *Consortium News*, May 20, 2015; and "Iran and North Korea," *Korea Times*, July 16, 2015.
363 "Iran be hich vajh ba korye shomali ghabel moghayeseh nist," [Iran and North Korea are Absolutely Incomparable] *Diyar Mirza News Agency*, January 6, 2015.

CONCLUSION

In addition to their likely intermittent interactions with Iranians in an-cient times, Koreans have managed to lay down, almost from scratch, the ground for significant connections to Iran in contemporary history. Strad-dling all military and diplomatic as well as economic and cultural realms, the Iran-based projects of Koreans have become a peculiar characteristic in Middle Eastern and East Asian international relations over the past decades. Moreover, the less detectable yet salient element of the international system has played a very pivotal role in smoothing the way for and accelerating the performance and accomplishment of Koreans from both sides of the Kore-an Peninsula in Iran. That is one compelling reason why some political and military aspects of Pyongyang–Tehran interactions have long been played up, while very little, if any, of South Korea's enormous economic and even cultural achievements in Iran have been publicized.

Of course, the communist regime of North Korea has been in contact with Iran primarily politically and militarily since the early 1980s. Not only there has been a great deal of surprise and bewilderment among stakeholders over the scope and duration of such delicate and often controversial connec-tions, their very initiation and onset were really unexpected in the first place. After all, the Islamic Republic had launched in 1979 its visionary platform of the "neither the East nor the West," with fierce anti-communist rhetoric and non-alignment proclivities. Even if the unforeseen outbreak of the Iran–Iraq War forced Tehran to turn to Pyongyang for arms during the 1980s, there was no serious impediment to an extension to that type of sensitive relationship in the aftermath of the eight-year-long bloody war. Each party had its own rationale, but it also had a lot to do with the way the international system dealt with both of them.

Although the North Korean political system had, from the get-go, been a nemesis for a large part of the international system, the Iranian one had just changed its affiliation. It went from being a darling of the international system into its bugbear. The DPRK belonged to the Soviet Union-led bloc during the Cold War, while it still preserved critically close connections, like an umbilical cord, to its giant communist neighbor, China, once the whole edifice of communism crumbled in Moscow and Eastern Europe. Because of its relatively small size and feeble capabilities, moreover, North Korea was not to be eventually perceived as a menacing threat to a new emerging pecking order in the international system. But the Iranian situation was rather a fine kettle of fish. In fact, the newly-established political system in Iran had taken issue with the international system's modus essendi, modus vivendi, and modus operandi. To the surprise of many stakeholders here and there, the Iranian braggart still did not come to its senses swiftly after it had to grapple with an eight-year long bloody war during which the vengeful retribution of the international system avowedly took its heavy toll on its unfortunate and hapless citizenry.

The international system, therefore, neither could make fast of the Iranian braggadocio once for all, nor would it put up with its precarious showmanship ungrudgingly. The Iranian incongruity was not to be rewarded by the gatekeepers of the international system, but the country was still given a wiggle room to muddle through. This is exactly what that brought the Iranian and North Korean political systems together to cooperate somewhat uninterruptedly both before and after the end of the Cold War. On top of that, the two wayward and anomalous political entities in Tehran and Pyongyang could be of some use to a new emerging division of labor within the international system by serving as a lightning rod of sorts. The Iranian–North Korean partnership subsequently became a frequent target of criticisms and negative claims of any type. By putting the spotlight on the Tehran–Pyongyang nexus, the major stakeholders in the new emerging international system could consolidate their own reshaping alliances and better vouchsafe the sedimented interests for part of which many besieged Iranian and North Korean citizens had been exacted a high price in one way or another.

Compared to their North Korean brethren, South Koreans could forge lesser politico-diplomatic and military ties with the Iranians. Although the ROK was far more successful than the DPRK in terms of building relatively friendly political connections to Tehran under the Pahlavi dynasty, however, South Koreans had to forgo a big part of this profitable bilateral relationship under the Islamic Republic, largely for external geopolitical and ideological reasons over which Seoul had little sway. In spite of such a disagreeable setback, South Korea managed to almost always keep a semblance of formal politico-diplomatic relations with the Persian Gulf country since the establishment of such ties in the early 1960s. The ROK scored relatively well in Iran in some other areas, without constructing a close political relationship with Tehran.

What particularly epitomizes that idiosyncrasy is South Korea's economic and technological inroads into the lives of Iranians in the absence of any meaningful affinity between the political capitals of the two countries. Koreans alone are certainly not to be given all the credit for this occurrence, as the tiny East Asian country greatly benefited from various external circumstances inimical to the interests of Iran and Iranians. Still, the size and scope of their economic accomplishments in, and technological encroachment upon, the Middle Eastern country really deserve scrutiny. South Korea's economic and technological presence in Iran has been truly phenomenal, at least over the past decade. This astonishing attainment can be sized up by any intelligible measure; from the sheer statistics on all Korean exports of manufactured products to Iran to the omnipresence of its top brands among the Iranian families and individual users of Korean automobiles, mobiles, and other electronic devices.

Meanwhile, the net result of South Koreans' economic and technological undertakings in Iran outstrips by far what their North Korean counterparts have been able to accomplish in Iran. The DPRK certainly engaged Iran in some purely economic fields, but even the material gains from such activity was hardly comparable to what the ROK pulled off. As a matter of fact, the net value of Pyongyang's overall dealings with Tehran, including missile and other military sales to Iran, was just still a fraction of what Seoul accomplished by shipping automobiles and electronic devices to Iran. On top of that, North Korea's transactions with Iran, whether the shipment of anti-missile tanks to Tehran in the mid-1980s or the imports of Iranian oil through China in the mid-2010s, were almost always the subject of close attention and publicity around the world, while South Korea escaped such scrutiny even when sending military equipment to Iran in the early 1980s.

Besides the realm of business and technology, South Koreans made progress among Iranians in the sphere of culture. Iran became one of the few foreign lands where the Hallyu products attracted exposure and public attention, far more than expected. The swift success achieved by a number of Hallyu dramas, despite the geographical distance and patent cultural differences between the two countries, surprised even cultural connoisseurs in South Korea. This unpredictable outcome was undoubtedly greatly assisted by a whole host of political and economic parameters mostly involving Iran. Even so, such shows had considerable impact upon the Iranian audience in one way or another. Additionally, the ROK's cultural publicity in Iran easily eclipsed what the DPRK had gained in the Iranian society simply because the imagined shared "political culture" between the communist state of North Korea and the Islamic Republic did not amount to much compared to the popularity of Hallyu products among their Iranian fans.

All in all, Koreans and their Iranian partners may still share business interests but they definitely have different dreams. South Koreans wish to rekindle their political ties to Tehran in order to secure and enhance their business; their cultural projects and soft projections in Iran have no higher objective. Needless to say, North Koreans are also maintaining their political and military interactions with Iran, by and large, in order to pave the way for more economic connections to Tehran.

Iran, however, is looking for a symbiotic relationship with Koreans from both sides of the peninsula. In order to partially make up for some of the lost, or mismanaged, opportunities in its multifaceted connections to the two Koreas, Iran seems to be aiming to reduce the political controversy in dealing with Pyongyang while striving to achieve a win-win situation in other bilateral interactions with Seoul. Since all the three parties are drifting in somewhat different directions, it would be very hard to predict the future of their dynamics.

Following is the declassified confidential report prepared for South Korea's President Syngman Rhee by the ROK's first goodwill mission to Iran in June 1957.

친선사절단 중동 및 아프리카
순방, 1957. 5. 1 - 6. 19

분류번호	724. 41 XA/XF
등록번호	119

색 인 목 록

분류번호	공류번호	생산과	생산년도	필름번호			화일	후대입번호	
				주제	번호	번호		시자	끝
774.4KWAF 1957	119	구미과	1957	C-001	B01	0001		~0202	

기능명칭 : 친선사절단 총율 및 이란(?)순방, 1957.6.1~6.19

감린번호	내 용	페이기
1	대통령 친서	0.0.0.4
2	결과보고	0.0.3.1
3	감사서한	0.1.9.9

138

- 103 -

Kabul, June 16, 1957

Your Excellency,

We arrived at Teheran, Iran, before noon of
June 5, and were met by the Inspector General of the
Iranian Air Force, a Brig. General Nassari, who
took us to the Royal Palace to sign the Guest Books
of the King and Queen, who were both away visiting
Spain and France. We were accommodated at the Iranian
Officers' Club. Shortly after we were installed at
the Club, the Foreign Ministry's Chief of Protocol,
a young man who was formerly with the Iranian Embassy
at Washington, came to pay his respects and express
welcome on behalf of the Iranian Government.

1. During our four day stay in Teheran, we
managed to see the Minister of Court, who received
us on behalf of the absent monarch; the Prime Minister,
ex-Minister of Court and Rector of the Teheran University; the Foreign Minister of United Nations
fame, Ali Gholi Ardalan; his Undersecretary, a dignified veteran diplomat in his late fifties; the War
Minister, a forti-ish energetic looking Major General;

152

- 104 -

and the Chief of JCS, a very dignified old warrior
with very correct and soldierly bearing. We met
the Prime Minister, the Foreign Minister and the
Chief of JCS only on the fourth day of our arrival
in Teheran, becaus e they were all away earlier for
the Bagdad Pact meeting at Karachi. The present
Prime Minister, Dr. Manuchehr Eghbal, is an energetic,
tough and taciturn man of action, who took over the
job from the present Minister of Court, Hussein
Ala, switching jobs with each other. Dr. Eghbal,
a Rught-wing Liberal, has had a wide experience of
government and, as a former rector of the Teheran
University, it is said that his appointment may
help to steady one important element of malcontents,
the intellectuals, who are said to be unhappy with
the irresponsible complacency of the fuling class
and with the commercial cativities of the royal
family (they own hotels, nightclubs and railways
as well as land). It is said, however, that nobody
in Teheran really thinks the new Prime Minister will
last long before he falls out with the Shah, who
is determined not to let any Premier acquire again

153

- 105 -

the dominating position of Dr. Mohammed Mossadegh.
They say that if Dr. Eghbal clashes with the Shah,
another yes-man will probably be appointed, and
this will lead to trouble, especially among the
intellectuals, in spite of all the good intentions
of the Shah, who is in his way doing his best to
improve the security and welfare of his people (one
evidence of this is the allocation of 60% of the
oil revenue to development programs).

2. All the officials we saw welcomed the visit
of my Mission, and expressed praise to Your Excellency
and our country's struggle against communists. This
sentiment has thus far been universal wherever we
went. Because of the general similarity of all the
interviews, I shall not attempt to describe them
all except for the one we had with the Minister of
Court. Hussein Ala was a very charming and venerable
old man of 70 with years of ambassadorial service
abroad. His present post is said to be as important
as the Prime Minister's because he not only advises
the King on important state affairs but also acts
as his representative when the sovereign becomes

154

unavailable, as was the case with us. He was indeed
a dapper old man with twinkling eyes, keen sense of
humour and flawless English. He received us in
his office at the Palace, shook hands warmly and welcomed the visit of the Mission on behalf of his
absent sovereign, saying that he was sure the King
would very much regret not having met us in person.
I gave him Your Excellency's letter and photograph
for transmission, and conveyed Your Excellency's
good wishes for the King, and the support at the
United Nations and for the recognition that Iran
had accorded our country, mentioning in addition
that of the ten countries that my Mission was visiting
and visited, Iran was the only one that had done so.
The old statesman asked me to convey his King's
appreciation to Your Excellency for the letter and
gift, saying that most probably the King would return
the compliment through the Iranian Embassy in Washington. He then said that he personally and the Iranian
people in general admired Your Excellency very much
as a great patriot and leader of the free world.
His people felt a special friendship and admiration

- 107 -

for our people, he said, and it was only natural for
his government to recognize the Republic of Korea
and to help ots cause at the United Nations. The
old Minister also said that at one time during the
Korean War the Iranian government had seriously
considered the idea of sending troops to participate
in the United Nation against the communist aggressors.
They were prevented from doing so merely by the constantly present threat posed by the proximity of the
Soviet Russians at their northern frontier, where
they shared a common border eith the Russians of over
one thousand miles. He said that they were fully
aware of the dangers of Russian communism, and therefore maintained a strong modernized army of about
200,000 men, aside from an air force of several
hundred pla nes, and a navy. He said that the Iranian
government's policy toward the Russians was to humour
them and avoid provoking them unnecessarily so long
as they showed friendliness to Iran. Recently,
he said, the Russians seemed to be bending backward
trying to please them; the decades old frontier dispute botween Russia and Iran had recently been settled

156

- 108 -

to the advantage of Iran.

3. The day before my Mission's departure from
Tehoran, the Minister of Defence gave a luncheon in
my honor. It was attended by the Minister of Court,
the Foreign Minister, his Undersecretary, the Chief
of the American Military Advisory Group (Maj. Gen.
Seitz), the Inspector General of the Iranian Air
Force, the Air Attache of the American Embassy,
and two other Iranian Officers, aside from the members
of my Mission.

4. Constitutional government was established
in Iran in 1906. Since that time executive power
has been exercised by a cabinet and officials acting
in the name of Shah. The legislature consists of
a two-house Parliament. By a constitutional amendment
of May 1949, the Shah was given the power to dissolve
the Parliament. Iran is among the richest oil-producing
countries. Other than oil, its principal exports
are cotton, carpets, fruits, gums, hides, wool,
opium, and rice. The Iranianrice is not glutinous
enough for our palate, but tastes alright otherwise.

5. While we were in Iran, we learned that at

- 109 -

the proposal of Soviet government there was a development program going on at Iran's northern frontier
that bordered Russia, under joint sponsorship
of the two governments but with Russia offering
the major portion of expenses. The program was for
developing irrigation and hydroelectric facilities.
It is said Russia is constantly offering gratuitous
technical aids and financial assistance, and Iran
has great difficulties in refusing most of them.
Japan seems to be doing quite well in Iran too.
She has initiated a joint development program for
fisheries industries along the Caspian Sea and the
Persian Gulf. She is said about to establish in
conjunction with the royal household a huge department store in Teheran with all modern facilities;
there is none in Iran at present. For the purpose
of improving the Iranian rechnuc of farming, the
Iranian government is said to have established an
immigration quota for Japanese farmers and their
families, with provisions of free grants of land.
I hear, however, that so far there are only five
Japanese farming families who were sufficiently

58

-- 110 --

attracted by the program to come to Iran.

5. ~~I was very much impressed with the city~~
of teheran. Like Bagdad, it was a pleasant
blend of old culture and efficient modernity. Its
streets are wide and clean with tall verdant trees
all along the streets and elsewhere. Being on
high elevation, averaging 4000 feet (this applies
to Iran in general), its air is refreshing and envi-
gorating. Its men and women almost uniformly handsome
and well built. Its streets full of modern cars
of all makes, and its shops filled with all sorts
of commodities.

We left Teheran in the morning of June 9.

With renewed assurances of my loyalty and esteem,

Yours respectfully,

LT. GEN. CHUNG YUL KIM .

His Excellency
The President,
. Kyung Mu Dai.

cc; The Foreign Minister

The Minister of Foreign Affairs

June 4, 1975

Excellency,

In view of the friendly ties existing between our two countries, the Imperial Government of Iran has decided to establish an Embassy in Seoul. I have the honour to introduce to Your Excellency H.E. Mr. Abdol-Amir Alam, Minister Counsellor, as Chargé d'Affaires of Iran to the Republic of Korea.

I would be grateful to Your Excellency for the cooperation and assistance which will be extended to H.E. Mr. A.A. Alam for the discharge of his duties.

Please accept, Excellency, the assurances of my highest consideration.

Yours sincerely,

Abbas Ali Khalatbary

His Excellency
Mr. Kim Dong Jo
Minister of Foreign Affairs
of the Republic of Korea
Seoul

IMPERIAL EMBASSY OF IRAN
SEOUL

September 2, 1975

P- 7

The Imperial Embassy of Iran presents its compliments to
the ministry of foreign affairs and has the honour to inform
the latter that as requested a copy of curriculum vitae of
H.E. Abdol Amir Alam Chargé d'affaires of Iran is herewith
forwarded for the ministry's requirement.

The Imperial Embassy of Iran avails itself of this
opportunity to renew to the ministry of foreign affairs the
assurances of its highest consideration.

Ministry of foreign affairs, Republic of Korea-Seoul

50

IMPERIAL EMBASSY OF IRAN
SEOUL

Curriculum Vitae
of
H.E. Abdol Amir Alam

Born in AHWAZ, Iran in the year 1918 where completed high school with a degree of diploma. Soon after admitted in Tehran University and graduated with B.A. degree in the fields of literature and political science. Received M.A. degree at Columbia and New York University in political science majoring in international law. Joined military service in 1939 for two years; first year at the military college and turned out as 2nd lieutenant officer for the second year. Entered ministry of foreign affairs in 1941 where obtained experiences in various departments; political, economic, administrative and cultural. Filled positions as member of supreme political council and head of conferences which the last one was an assignment before arriving Seoul. Assignments abroad followed as vice consul at the consulate general of Iran in New York, Counselor at the Imperial Embassy of Iran in Japan and the last Chargé d'affaires of Iran.

51

اداره ـــ تشریفات
شماره ـــ ۴۱۸۰۶۱۱
تاریخ ـــ ۲۵۴۰۱
پیوست ـــ

وزارت امورخارجه

یـادداشـت

تشریفات وزارت امورخارجه شاهنشاهی با اظهار تعارفات خودبــه
سفارت جمهوری کره احتراما عطف بهیادداشت شماره۷۵-۳- C / KIR
مورخ سوم مارس ۱۹۷۵ در خصوص دعوت جناب آقای KUCHA-CHUN
شهردار سئول از شهردار پایتخت وهمسرشان برای بازدید ازجمهوری کــره
اشعارمیدارد .

جناب آقای نیک پی دعوت مذکور رابا اظهار امتنان پذیرفته وتاریــخ
۸ الی ۱۲ سپتامبره۱۹۷۵ رابرای انجام این مسافرت پیشنهاد نموده اند .

موجب امتنان خواهدبود چنانچه تاریخ مذکور رابه اطلاع جناب آقــای
شهردار سئول رسانده وازهرنظری که دراین مورد دارند تشریفات وزارت امـور
خارجه رامستحضرفرمایند .

موقع رابرای تجدید احترامات فائقه مغتنم میشمارد .

سفارت جمهوری کره ـ تهران

MINISTRY OF FOREIGN AFFAIRS

Protocol Dept.
No. 1182/11
Date 54/1/31 (April 20, 75)

NOTE

The Protocol of the Ministry of Foreign Affairs presents its compliments to the Embassy of the Republic of Korea and referring to the latter's Note No. KIR/C-3-75 dated March 3, 1975, regarding the invitation made by His Excellency Mr. Kucha-Chun, the Mayor of Seoul, to the Mayor of Tehran and Madame Gholamreza Nikpay to visit the Republic of Korea, has the honour to inform the latter as follows.

His Excellency Mr. Nikpay and Madame have accepted the mentioned invitation with pleasure and the suggested date for their visit from Korea is from Sep. 8 to Sep. 12, 1975.

It would be appreciated if that Embassy informs the above mentioned suggested date to His Excellency Mayor of Seoul and then inform the Imperial Ministry from the result.

The Imperial Ministry of Foreign Affairs avails itself of this opportunity to renew to the Embassy the assurances of its highest consideration.

Embassy of the Rep. of Korea-Tehran

OFFICE OF THE MAYOR

SEOUL METROPOLITAN GOVERNMENT

SEOUL, KOREA

June 18, 1976

The Honorable Gholamreza Nikpay
Mayor of Tehran
Empire of Iran

Sir:

I have received a letter from the Korean Ambassador to the Empire of Iran, informing me of your intention to visit Korea.

I wish to formally invite you and Mrs. Nikpay accompanied by about two members of your entourage to visit Seoul, the capital of the Republic of Korea, for four days, from 22nd to 25th March 1977.

Under this invitation, the airline tickets and hotel charges will be borne by this city.

I firmly believe that your visit of Seoul will further enhance the friendly ties between our two countries and the friendship established between our two cities through my visit of Tehran in 1975.

Welcoming your forthcoming visit to Seoul from the bottom of my heart, I remain

Yours truly,

Koo, Jachoon

Koo, Ja Choon
Mayor

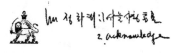

IMPERIAL EMBASSY OF IRAN
SEOUL

May 24, 1977

No. 235

The Imperial Embassy of Iran presents its
compliments to the Ministry of Foreign Affairs,
Republic of Korea, and has the honour to inform
you that by invitation of Hon. Koo Ja Choon,
Mayor of Seoul, Hon. Gholamreza Nikpay, Mayor of
Tehran and Mrs. Nikpay and two other member of
the Tehran municipality will arrive in Seoul on
Sunday 26, 1977 by Flight No. KE 001 for a five
day visit.

The Imperial Embassy of Iran avails itself
of this opportunity to renew to the Ministry of
Foreign Affairs, Republic of Korea, the assurances
of its highest consideration.

Ministry of Foreign Affairs,
Republic of Korea,
Seoul.

SEOUL METROPOLITAN GOVERNMENT
SEOUL, KOREA

Meritorious Service Record

1. Mr. Javad Shahrestani, Mayor of Tehran, assumed his office
in August 1977, succeeding to his predecessor, former Mayor Nikpay.
In order to enhance the friendship between Seoul and Tehran, capital
cities of our two countries, his predecessor had reached agreement to
exchange the designation of streets in Seoul and Tehran. For this
goodwill event, he invited Ja Choon Koo, Mayor of Seoul, to visit his
city (November 26 to 29, 1977) and formally christened the "Seoul
Street" in Tehran. This event marked an opportunity of consolidating
the existing friendship between Seoul and Tehran. Mayor Shahrestani
is known as one of those Iranian leaders who are extremely in favor
of the Republic of Korea.

2. During his tenure as the Road and Transportation Minister,
he also actively rendered his assistance to Korean construction
companies in starting business in Iran.

BIBLIOGRAPHY

Alexander, Kern. *Economic Sanctions: Law and Public Policy*. New York: Palgrave Macmillan, 2009.

Azad, Shirzad. "Iran and the Two Koreas: A Peculiar Pattern of Foreign Policy." *The Journal of East Asian Affairs* 26, no. 2 (2012): 163–192.

———. "Déjà vu Diplomacy: South Korea's Middle East Policy under Lee Myung-bak." *Contemporary Arab Affairs* 6, no. 4 (November 2013): 552–566.

———. *Koreans in the Persian Gulf: Policies and International Relations*. Abingdon and New York: Routledge, 2015.

———. "Principlism Engages Pragmatism: Iran's Relations with East Asia under Ahmadinejad." *Asian Politics & Policy* 7, no. 4 (October 2015): 555–573.

Beal, Tim. *North Korea: The Struggle against American Power*. London: Pluto Press, 2005.

Bell, Daniel A. *Beyond Liberal Democracy: Political Thinking for an East Asian Context*. Princeton, NJ: Princeton University Press, 2006.

Cronin, Patrick M., ed. *Double Trouble: Iran and North Korea as Challenges to International Security*. Westport, CT: Praeger Security International, 2008.

Dobson, Alan P. *US Economic Statecraft for Survival 1933–1991: Of Sanctions, Embargoes and Economic Warfare*. London and New York: Routledge, 2002.

Drury, A. Cooper. *Economic Sanctions and Presidential Decisions: Models of Political Rationality*. New York: Palgrave Macmillan, 2005.

Duncan, John B. *The Origins of the Choson Dynasty*. Seattle, WA: The University of Washington Press, 2014.

Duus, Peter. *The Abacus and the Sword: The Japanese Penetration of Korea, 1895–1910.* Berkeley: University of California Press, 1995.

Eyler, Robert. *Economic Sanctions: International Policy and Political Economy at Work.* New York: Palgrave Macmillan, 2007.

Farber, David R. *Taken Hostage: The Iran Hostage Crisis and America's First Encounter with Radical Islam.* Princeton, NJ: Princeton University Press, 2005.

Fenollosa, Ernest F. *Epochs of Chinese and Japanese Art: An Outline History of East Asiatic Design.* Berkeley, CA: Stone Bridge Press, 2007.

Financial Times, The. *Financial Times Oil and Gas International Year Book.* London: Longman, 1983.

French, Paul. *North Korea: The Paranoid Peninsula — A Modern History*, second edition. London and New York: Zed Books, 2007.

Gause, Ken E. *North Korea under Kim Chong-il: Power, Politics, and Prospects for Change.* Santa Barbara, California: Praeger, 2011.

Gosfield, Frank, and Bernhardt J. Hurwood. *Korea: Land of the 38th Parallel.* New York: Parents' Magazine Press, 1969.

Griffis, William Elliot. *Corea, Without and Within: Chapters on Corean History, Manners and Religion with Hendrick Hamel's Narrative of Captivity and Travels in Corea, annotated.* Philadelphia: Presbyterian Board of Publication, 1885.

Hemmert, Martin. *Tiger Management: Korean Companies on World Markets.* Abingdon and New York: Routledge, 2012.

Hershock, Peter D., and Roger T. Ames. eds. *Confucian Cultures of Authority.* Albany, NY: State University of New York Press, 2006.

Hollym International Corporation. *Cultural Treasures of Korea: National Treasures 2: Ancient Tomb Relics, Ceramics, Handicraft Arts.* Seoul: Hollym International Corporation, 1993.

Houghton, David Patrick. *US Foreign Policy and the Iran Hostage Crisis.* New York: Cambridge University Press, 2004.

Hundt, David. *Korea's Developmental Alliance.* Abingdon and New York: Routledge, 2009.

Hunter, Robert E. *Building Security in the Persian Gulf.* Santa Monica, CA: RAND, 2010.

Huntley, Wade L. "Rebels without a Cause: North Korea, Iran and the NPT." *International Affairs* 82, no. 4 (2006): 723–742.

Jackson, Robert J., and Philip Towle. *Temptations of Power: The United States in Global Politics after 9/11*. New York: Palgrave Macmillan, 2006.

Jones, F.C. *The Far East: A Concise History*. London: Pergamon Press, 1966.

Kemp, Geoffrey. "U.S.–Iranian Strategic Cooperation since 1979." In *Checking Iran's Nuclear Ambitions*, edited by Henry Sokolski and Patrick Clawson. Washington, DC: Strategic Studies Institute, 2004.

Lane, George. *Early Mongol Rule in Thirteenth-Century Iran: A Persian Renaissance.* London and New York: RoutledgeCurzon, 2003.

Lemke, Douglas. *Regions of War and Peace*. New York: Cambridge University Press, 2002.

Lennon, Alexander T.J., and Camille Eiss. eds. *Reshaping Rogue States: Preemption, Regime Change, and U.S. Policy toward Iran, Iraq, and North Korea*. Cambridge, MA: The MIT Press, 2004.

Levin, Norman D. *The Shape of Korea's Future: South Korean Attitudes Toward Unification and Long-Term Security Issues*. Santa Monica, CA: RAND, 1999.

Litwak, Robert S. "Living with Ambiguity: Nuclear Deals with Iran and North Korea." *Survival: Global Politics and Strategy* 50, no. 1 (2008): 91–118.

Mason, Mike. *Global Shift: Asia, Africa, and Latin America, 1945–2007*. Montreal & Kingston: McGill-Queen's University Press, 2013.

McNamara, Dennis L., ed. *Corporatism and Korean Capitalism*. London and New York: Routledge, 1999.

Ministry of Culture and Sports. *Religious Culture in Korea*. Seoul: Ministry of Culture and Sports, Religious Affairs Office, 1996.

Ministry of Foreign Affairs, Republic of Korea. *Daehan minguk wegyo yeonpyo* [Republic of Korea, Annual Report on Foreign Policy]. Seoul: Ministry of Foreign Affairs, 1970.

Ministry of Foreign Affairs, Republic of Korea. *Wegyo Munseo* [Diplomatic Archives]. Seoul: Republic of Korea, Ministry of Foreign Affairs, 1994.

Noland, Marcus. *Avoiding the Apocalypse: The Future of the Two Koreas*. Washington, DC: Institute for International Economics, 2000.

Olsen, Harald. "South Korea's Pivot toward Iran: Resource Diplomacy and ROK–Iran Sanctions." *The Korean Journal of Defense Analysis* 25, no. 1 (March 2013): 73–85.

Onians, John. *Atlas of World Art*. Oxford University Press, 2004.

Pack, Howard. "Asian Successes VS. Middle Eastern Failures: The Role of Technology Transfer in Economic Development." *Issues in Science and Technology* XXIV, no, 3 (Spring 2008): 47–54.

Park, Chung-hee. *Kunggawa hydngmydngiwa na* [The Country, the Revolution, and I]. Seoul: Hyangmunsa, 1963.

Pirie, Iain. *The Korean Developmental State: From Dirigisme to Neo-liberalism.* Abingdon and New York: Routledge, 2008.

Potter, Lawrence G. *The Persian Gulf in History.* New York: Palgrave Macmillan, 2009.

Robinson, David M. *Empire's Twilight: Northeast Asia under the Mongols.* Cambridge, MA: The Harvard University Asia Center, 2009.

Rowen, Henry S., ed. *Behind East Asian Growth: The Political and Social Foundations of Prosperity.* London and New York: Routledge, 1998.

Sagan, Scott. Kenneth N. Waltz, and Richard K. Betts. "A Nuclear Iran: Promoting Stability or Courting Disaster?" *Journal of International Affairs* 60, no. 2 (Spring 2007): 135–150.

Shawcross, William. *The Shah's Last Ride: The Story of the Exile, Misadventures and Death of the Emperor.* New York: Touchstone, 1989.

Wilson, Rodney. *Economic Development in the Middle East.* London and New York, 1995.

Wright, Steven. *The United States and Persian Gulf Security: The Foundations of the War on Terror.* Reading, Berkshire: Ithaca Press, 2007.

INDEX

Numerals

38th parallel, 3, 12
5+1 party, 10, 34, 35, 37, 47, 48

A

Abe, Shinzo, 39
Academy Award for Best Foreign Language Film, 126
Academy of Motion Picture Arts and Sciences, 126
actors and actresses, pro-Korean influence in Iran, 111, 117, 121, 124, 126
Afghanistan, 29, 63
Ahmadinejad, Mahmoud, 29, 31, 34, 46, 62, 64, 65, 67-69, 73, 77, 78, 106
alcohol, 103
Alexander, 31, 65, 99
alliance politics, 15, 23
anti-communism, 15, 18, 133
Arab countries, 8, 18, 23, 40, 42, 44-46, 56, 57, 60, 70, 73, 99, 113
arms trade, 19-21, 42, 50, 95, 133
Asan Institute for Policy Studies (Asan cheongchaeg yeonguwon), 45
axis of evil, 8, 28, 30, 31

B

Baghdad, 20, 21
banks, Korean banks and Iran, 66, 69, 70, 80
barter system, 95, 96

beauty drain, 118
black market, 4, 69, 80, 81
blockbuster, 109
blocked funds, 68, 70
bonanza, 19, 34, 36, 38, 55, 60, 106
brain drain, 61, 118
British American Tobacco, 74
Bush, George W., 8, 27-29, 63

C

capital drain, 118
Cauli, 12
Central Asia, 11
CF Crystal, 51
chaebol, 6, 8, 114, 117
"Children of Heaven", 126
China, 7, 8, 10-16, 20, 21, 24, 34, 35, 37, 51-54, 63, 64, 66, 67, 70, 72, 73, 77, 79, 88, 89, 92, 95, 107, 117, 119, 121, 134, 136
chivalry, 119
Choson (see Joseon)
Christian principles, 97
cigarettes, 74, 101
Coca-Cola, 101
commercialization, 99
commodification, 99
communism, 134
competition, 43, 92, 126
conglomerates (chaebols), 6
construction, 4, 17, 55-57, 60, 64, 88
cosmetic surgery, 111
cultural influence of Korea in Iran, 39, 102, 125, 129

D

Dae Jang Geum, 107
decadence vs. traditional values, 101, 125
demilitarized zone (DMZ), 5, 49
democracy, 29, 58
denuclearization, 40, 47, 48, 96
Daewoo Shipbuilding, 88
diaspora, Iranian, 101, 124, 131
Dong-A Ilbo, 50, 57, 73, 74, 108
DPRK (North Korea)
    and China, 20, 24, 51-54, 63, 89, 95, 134, 136
    and Iran, 3, 6, 8, 19, 20, 24, 25, 28, 29, 47, 93-95, 128-131, 133-135
    and Iraq, 28
    and the Middle East, 20
    and ROK, 21, 30, 32, 93, 135, 136
divorce, 118
documentary, 117
drought, 26
drug addicts, 79, 118
dual containment, 27, 63, 65
Dubai, 8, 45

E

East China Sea, 51, 52, 54
Eastern Europe, 134
economic development, 15, 29, 63, 77, 91, 96, 98, 110, 113
economic diplomacy, 39, 127
education, 6, 58, 80, 83, 101, 104, 105
Egypt, 18, 23, 56
entertainment, 104, 109, 111, 120
espionage, 18
Esse cigarettes, 74, 75
European Union (EU), 35, 37, 38, 68, 70, 86, 100, 134

F

fertility rate, 87
finance, 4, 55, 59, 69, 88
France, 10, 34, 35, 38

G

Germany, 10, 34, 56, 57, 64

Girls Generation, 112
goodwill mission by Korea, 14, 137
Goryeo dynasty, 12
Great Britain, 10, 12, 13, 15, 27, 34, 35, 62, 65, 77, 99, 129
gross domestic product (GDP), 93
Gulf Cooperation Council (GCC), 23, 44, 45

H

Hallyu (Korean wave in entertainment), 9, 10, 107-117, 119, 120, 122-125, 136
Hanwha Total, 52
Hashemi Rafsanjani, Akbar, 20, 62-64, 106
heritage, 13, 84, 85, 100, 103, 123, 129
hermit kingdom, 112
higher education, 6, 80, 101
Hollywood, 101, 126
Hong Kong, 54
Huawei Technologies Co., 91
Hussein, Saddam, 28, 29
Hwanung, 11
Hyundai Motor Company, 8, 40, 57, 72, 74, 91, 92, 115

I

ibn Hayyan, Jabir, 14
ibn Khordadbeh, Abulqasim, 12
imports mafia, 77-79, 115-117, 123
industrialization, 15, 56, 58, 59, 83, 90, 98, 110, 113, 114, 122, 123
inflation, 118
insurgency, 29
intermediaries, 12, 13, 21, 66
international system, 9, 10, 17, 19, 23, 35, 93, 133, 134
internet, 69, 92, 101, 107, 109
Iran
    American hostage crisis in, 8, 18, 65, 68
    Chamber of Commerce, Industries, Mines and Agriculture, 72, 73
    Europe's relations with, 36
    historical influence on Korea, 12
    Islamic Japan" as a development concept, 85, 86
    and China, 7, 53, 54, 63, 66, 79, 88, 92, 117, 119, 136

O

Obama, Barack, 38, 66-68
oil shock, 55, 70, 71
Operation Eagle Claw, 8

P

Pahlavi dynasty, 4, 16, 17, 24, 45, 60, 61, 84, 85, 100, 102, 105, 135
Park Chung-hee, 38, 58, 59
Park Geun-hye, and expanding ties, 12, 38, 87, 125
Persia, early influence of, 12, 13
Persian language, 57, 120, 121
plastic surgery, 49, 111-
political culture, presumed affinity, 9, 129-131, 136
pornography, 101
prostitution, 103
Protestant Ethic and the Spirit of Capitalism, The, 97
publicity, 9, 110, 115, 116, 123, 128, 136

Q

Qajar, 100
quid pro quo, 66

R

rapprochement, 22, 41
reciprocity, 128
reconstruction, 23, 27, 62, 63, 106
refinery, 61
religion, 12
Republic of China (ROC, Taiwan), 15, 16, 36, 64, 102
ROK (South Korea)
  and Arab countries, 16, 23, 44
  and diplomatic relations with Iran, 124
  and the USA, 23, 26, 33, 41
resistance economy, 82, 116
reunification, 51
Roh Moo-hyun, 30
Roosari diplomacy, 39, 127
Rouhani, Hassan, 34, 36, 47, 48, 64, 69, 88, 89, 96, 118, 128
Revolutionary Guards, 25, 50, 54
Russia, 10, 21, 23, 26, 34, 66, 95, 134

S

sales diplomacy, 38, 39
Samguk Yusa (*Legends and History of the Three Kingdoms*), 11
Samsung Group, 8, 72-76, 91, 93, 115, 119
Sanchi, sinking of, 51-54
sanctions, 21, 27, 30-38, 41, 47, 50, 52, 53, 57, 62, 63, 65-70, 74-80, 88, 117, 118, 130
Sassanian Empire, 13
satellites, 101, 107
Saudi Arabia, 44, 45, 57, 60, 70
second boom for ROK, 40, 87
"second Japan", 85
security alliance, 18, 32
security umbrella, 43
Seoul Metropolitan Government, 105
Seoul National University, 42, 113
Seoul Street, 105
September 11, 81
sexuality, 103, 125
Shah (see Pahlavi)
Silk Road, 12
Silla, 12
sisterhood, 105
smartphones, 75
smuggling, 73, 77, 80-82
soft power, 98, 99, 102, 104, 125, 127, 128
Southeast Asia, 74
sovereignty, 48, 116
Soviet Union, 21, 26, 95
sponsorship, 116
Ssangyang Corporation, 61, 74
suitcase trade, 81

T

Taegukgi, 13, 14
taekwondo, 109
Taipei, 15, 37
Taiwan, 15, 16, 36, 64, 102
Tang dynasty, 13
Tangun, 11
technology (see also missile programs), 3, 4, 25, 59, 89-92, 94, 123, 136
technology transfer, 90, 91
Teheran-ro (Tehran Street), 105
Tel Aviv, 45

Printed in the United States
By Bookmasters